Words of Praise for INSIDE U

"Grandmaster Yu's journey to the highest level of martial arts expertise is a life lesson for all of us, as he shares his inspirational message of overcoming adversity with courage, perseverance, and spirituality."
— **Alan F. Horn,** president and COO of Warner Bros. Films

"I had the pleasure of meeting Byong Yu in 1965 when he came to the United States as a member of the Korean Tae Kwon Do demonstration team. That meeting grew into a friendship. Knowing Grandmaster Byong Yu now for over 37 years, I can say with confidence that he is one of the supreme martial artists in the world. It's an honor to call him a friend."
— **Chuck Norris,** actor

"My career has been greatly enhanced by the things I have learned about myself through martial arts training with Master Yu. **Inside U** *gives those not fortunate enough to be able to train and study with Master Yu access through this book to his limitless supply of knowledge, wisdom, and secrets of maintaining good mental, physical, and spiritual health."*
— **Stanley Clarke,** Grammy-winning, Emmy-nominated musician, composer, and recording artist

"Master Yu's training and inspiration over the past five years has encouraged me to raise my levels of self-confidence and motivation.
I will always be indebted to him."
— **Michael Klausman,** president, CBS Studio Center

"I put Byong Yu in the same category with Bruce Lee. These are extraordinary people who devoted their entire lives to martial arts."
— **Stirling Silliphant,**
Academy Award–winning screenwriter of *In the Heat of the Night*

"Being a student of Master Yu has increased my ability to focus and concentrate and has enhanced my discipline. He has also given me a greater understanding of the relationship between my mind, body, and spirit. Master Yu's teachings have been beneficial to both my professional and personal life."
— **Jennifer Garner,** motion picture *(Daredevil)* and TV *(Alias)* star

*"**Inside U** unfolds as an autobiographical journey of Master Yu's knowledge and quest for wisdom. Page by page, chapter by chapter, there are overt and subtle signposts for us to read within the context of this riveting story of Master Yu's life. Once you pick up this book and begin to read it, it is difficult to put down until finished."*
— **Mark L. Gordon, M.D.,** chairman, Millennium Anti-Aging Medicine Group

"The gripping journey through Grandmaster Byong Yu's life serves as a template from which we can fashion our own lives. From [the time he was] a young boy he faced many challenges. Through his martial arts training, he sculpted his body, mind, and spirit to become a great martial artist. His accomplishments are an inspiration. Grandmaster Yu has continually passed on his wisdom and knowledge to his students, and now through this book, to the rest of the world."
— **Gerard J. Fasel, Ph.D.,**
professor of physics and mathematics, Pepperdine University

Inside U

hay house
Titles of Related Interest

BOOKS

An Attitude of Gratitude: *21 Life Lessons,* by Keith D. Harrell

Every Move You Make: *Bodymind Exercises to Transform Your Life,*
by Nikki Winston

Flex Ability: *A Story of Strength and Survival,*
by Flex Wheeler, with Cindy Pearlman

It's Not about the Horse: *It's about Overcoming Fear and Self-Doubt,*
by Wyatt Webb, with Cindy Pearlman

10 Secrets for Success and Inner Peace, by Dr. Wayne W. Dyer

CARD DECKS

Healing the Mind and Spirit Cards, by Brian L. Weiss, M.D.

Manifesting Good Luck Cards: *Growth and Enlightenment,*
by Deepak Chopra

Wisdom Cards, by Louise L. Hay

Zen Cards, by Daniel Levin

Please visit the Hay House USA Website at: **www.hayhouse.com;**
the Hay House Australia Website at: **www.hayhouse.com.au;**
or the Hay House U.K. Website at: **www.hayhouse.co.uk**

Inside U

How to Become a Master of Your Own Destiny

Grandmaster Byong Yu, Ph.D.

with Tom Bleecker

Hay House, Inc.

Carlsbad, California • Sydney, Australia • London, U.K.
Canada • Hong Kong

Published and distributed in the United States by: Hay House, Inc., P.O. Box 5100, Carlsbad, CA 92018-5100 • *Phone:* (760) 431-7695 or (800) 654-5126 • *Fax:* (760) 431-6948 or (800) 650-5115 • www.hayhouse.com • **Published and distributed in Australia by:** Hay House Australia, Ltd., 18/36 Ralph St., Alexandria NSW 2015 • *Phone:* 612-9669-4299 • *Fax:* 612-9669-4144 • www.hay-house.com.au • **Published and Distributed in the United Kingdom by:** Hay House UK, Ltd. • Unit 202, Canalot Studios • 222 Kensal Rd., London W10 5BN • *Phone:* 44-20-8962-1230 • *Fax:* 44-20-8962-1239 • www.hayhouse.co.uk • **Distributed in Canada by:** Raincoast • 9050 Shaughnessy St., Vancouver, B.C. V6P 6E5 • *Phone:* (604) 323-7100 • *Fax:* (604) 323-2600

Editorial supervision: Jill Kramer • *Design:* Amy Rose Szalkiewicz
Interior photos: Courtesy of Grandmaster Byong Yu

The author of this book does not dispense medical advice or prescribe the use of any technique as a form of treatment for physical or medical problems without the advice of a physician, either directly or indirectly. The intent of the author is only to offer information of a general nature to help you in your quest for emotional and spiritual well-being. In the event you use any of the information in this book for yourself, which is your constitutional right, the author and the publisher assume no responsibility for your actions.

Library of Congress Cataloging-in-Publication Data

Yu, Byong, 1935-
Inside you / Master Byong Yu with Tom Bleecker.
p. cm.
ISBN 1-4019-0212-X (tradepaper) • 1-4019-0211-1 (hardcover)
1. Yu, Byong, 1935- 2. Martial artists—Korea—Biography. I. Bleecker, Tom. II. Title.
GV1113.Y8A3 2003
796.8'092—dc21

2002151516

Hardcover ISBN 1-4019-0211-1
Tradepaper ISBN 1-4019-0212-X

06 05 04 03   4 3 2 1
1st printing, August 2003

Printed in the United States of America

Courage

Fear not!
Strive to take the high road
Though difficult and rough.
Those of the past who achieved greatness
Devoted themselves thusly.

Fear not!
Though your future
With painful effort is achieved.
Stretch forth your hands
And grasp the goal.

Go on—go on!
With mightiness of will
With the power or courage.
Thus in the way of Yong Do
Will you be led to hope and happiness,
Driving away the devil of fear.

— Grandmaster Byong Yu

CONTENTS

PREFACE

I have spent 63 years studying, practicing, and teaching the martial arts—ever since I was five years old. Over the years, I have often said that if the only reason I devoted my entire life to the martial arts was to ensure my physical safety, then I have made a horrible investment of time. You see, one doesn't have to spend 63 years studying the martial arts to learn self-defense. I knew how to adequately protect myself after training for two years.

There is much more to the martial arts than learning how to block, kick, and punch. Besides the obvious physical benefits, my many years of continual training have been a vehicle through which I ultimately achieved a higher spiritual level.

For all of us, life is a journey. My personal path has been one of an infinite number of routes that all headed to the same destination. After more than six decades of suiting up in my martial arts uniform, I have come to recognize that the life lessons I have learned are the same as those learned by the non-martial artist. It isn't necessary that you, the reader, go through 60 years of rugged martial arts training in order to benefit from what I have discovered. If you happen to be a martial artist, that's fine. But if you're not, that's fine, too—I have already completed six decades of blocking, kicking, and punching for you.

My main motivation for sharing my life with you is to add immeasurably to your life. If you take the time to learn from my mistakes and successes, and apply to your life the lessons that are contained in this book, then I'm confident that together we can achieve that end.

INTRODUCTION

Life is neither a random event nor a colossal cosmic joke. There *is* a definite purpose to our existence, and in order to accomplish it, the universe has given us a physical body and a limited span of time.

Our lives were never meant to run on autopilot. As we travel along our journey, we soon discover that what we make, or don't make, of our life is entirely up to us.

The universe doesn't want us to fail at anything, because when we fail, it fails. By design we are meant to succeed at everything we set out to accomplish. Nothing is more pleasing to the universe than that we live to see our every dream become reality. I hope that as you read this book, you will see that my life has very clearly illustrated this fact.

Inside U is divided into two parts. The first focuses on my life.

At an early age, I was diagnosed by doctors as mentally retarded, labeled by my mother as a "crying baby," and later nicknamed "Ugly Boy" by the neighborhood kids who made fun of my disabilities and threw rocks at me. Through these hardships, however, I made four crucial discoveries that dramatically changed my life: (1) I was born into this world with a specific destiny that I am meant to fulfill; (2) in my quest to fulfill my destiny I would be handed many crosses to bear along the way; (3) my bearing of these crosses would lead to life lessons that result in the growth and advancement of who and what I am; and (4) although I sometimes may not recognize it, I never face a problem in life that doesn't have a positive result already waiting for me. The day I came to this realization, every negative emotion inside me was greatly lessened, and since then I've never felt alone.

The second part of this book clearly defines the practical, working tools that I've attained from more than 60 years of studying and teaching the martial arts, coupled with the Eastern philosophy that is an integral part of my Asian heritage. If you take the time to learn these fundamental principles and apply them to your daily living, your life will be enriched beyond your wildest dreams.

I would like to close with a note about God. While I am not a believer in or follower of organized religion, I do believe in a Superior Being. Because of my martial arts background, my religious beliefs lean toward Taoism. That said, I feel it is extremely important during our lifetime to establish a satisfactory understanding and relationship with whatever our definition of "God" may turn out to be.

Through the course of my life, I've discovered that my concept of a Superior Being was for many years far too small. Never was this better illustrated than when I heard a five-year-old girl give her definition of heaven. After a thoughtful silence, she said that at night she looked up at the stars and envisioned the earth surrounded by a huge black veil, and that each star represented a pinhole in the veil that gave us only a tiny glimpse of what existed on the other side, which was heaven.

Isn't that beautiful? While keeping that little girl's definition of heaven in mind and spirit, I hope that you will come away from our time together not only reaching for the stars, but reaching *beyond* them to the heaven inside you.

Let us begin.

(**Note:** Many of you may wonder why there are so many dragons pictured throughout this book. The reason is that in the Asian culture, dragons have considerable influence over the lives of the people they guide. *Inside U* is a vehicle through which the good dragon will lead you along a path to a peaceful and fulfilling life.)

PART I

Defeat
and
Victory

chapter 1

Ugly Boy

:::
:::

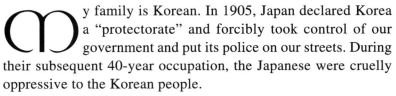

y family is Korean. In 1905, Japan declared Korea a "protectorate" and forcibly took control of our government and put its police on our streets. During their subsequent 40-year occupation, the Japanese were cruelly oppressive to the Korean people.

Prior to meeting my mother, my father, Kwan, attended a Japanese college, where he received a bachelor's degree and graduated with honors. He returned to Korea and applied for a teaching position at the University of Korea. However, his application was rejected because of his brother's involvement with the revolutionary movement based in Manchuria, which had resulted in their family name being red-tagged by the Japanese. Refusing to give up, my father applied for teaching positions at the high school and junior high school levels, but was again turned down. Sadly, his application was even turned down at the elementary school level.

Shortly thereafter, Father took a menial labor job working in a bakery that was owned by my maternal grandfather. It was there that my father met my mother, Ik, when they both were in their mid-20s.

From an early age, my mother wanted to be a singer and dancer, but such occupations were frowned upon as being low class, so she ended up pursing a career as an elementary school teacher instead. After marrying my father, she gave birth to my brother, Duk; my sister, Sun; and me.

I was born in the small village of Kyung Ki-Do on January 17, 1935. It was a terrible time for Korean couples to be having children, for during this time, Japan siphoned off more and more of Korea's resources in order to feed its Imperial war machine. Large quantities of rice were exported to Japan, which left Koreans facing a serious food shortage. Our standard of living deteriorated, and hundreds of thousands of our farmers were forced to move to Manchuria or Japan, where they endured conditions that weren't any better.

The Japanese tried to break the Korean backbone by implementing a policy to assimilate the citizens of Korea into the Japanese culture. People were forced to adopt Japanese names and convert to Japan's native religion of Shinto, use of the Korean language in schools and businesses was forbidden, and wearing traditional Korean clothing was discouraged. Moreover, the Japanese wanted Korean men to marry Japanese women. As for Korean women, more than 200,000—ages 12 to 35, both married and unmarried—were forced into prostitution. Most serviced as many as 20 to 30 soldiers a day. Those who were unfortunate enough to become pregnant were killed.

The Japanese occupation brought a tremendous sadness to Korea. I still recall that the birds sat in the trees instead of flying, and they rarely sang.

Shortly after my birth, our family moved to Ansung (about 30 miles from Seoul), where we shared a ramshackle four-room wooden house with three other families. We had no telephone, electricity, or indoor plumbing. A small wood-burning stove was all we had to get us through the harsh winters, and our toilet was a large metal drum half-buried in the backyard.

The children in our home wore hand-me-downs and had a few hand-made toys—only the Japanese and a small number of Koreans who worked for them could afford to purchase real toys for their children. The kids in my neighborhood played card games, with decks we would cut from cardboard and draw pictures and numbers on. We also collected round stones from the river and played several board games such as checkers. "Kick the can" was another favorite pastime.

I knew at an early age that something was physically wrong with me, for I seemed different from my siblings. Until the age of three, I couldn't coordinate my arms and legs. When people would extend their arms to pick me up, I would just stare at them. I could see their outstretched arms and understand what they wanted, but by the time I reached out to them, they had turned and walked away. My mental connection to my outer world worked in slow motion.

I didn't talk until I was five. I could hear, I could think, but I couldn't speak. Instead, I communicated with hand gestures and a gibberish that only my parents understood. Although I had great difficulty with verbal communication, my mind was intact. I understood people around me— they (other than my parents) just couldn't understood me.

The day came when my mother and father took me to a local clinic, where doctors diagnosed me as mentally retarded. They explained to my parents that even when I reached adulthood I wouldn't be able to care for myself and would be a lifelong burden to the family. I still remember hearing one of the doctors tell my mother that she should focus her attention and efforts on my brother and sister—she should simply put me in a corner and let me die. These doctors concluded that because I couldn't talk, I couldn't understand the spoken word, or because I couldn't coordinate my hands and legs, I couldn't think.

Many years later I asked my mother about our visit to the clinic because it continued to haunt me. Tears fell from her eyes, and after a long pause, she said, "Yes, your father and I thought you couldn't survive. If we died, what would you do? Who would take care of you? The doctor said it might be best if we just allowed you to die. That way we wouldn't be burdened by it all, and your brother and sister wouldn't be burdened either—and yourself, you wouldn't be forced to live a life of torment and would rest in peace."

As inhumane as this sounds, during the Japanese occupation, disabled Korean children were often abandoned. The parents basically isolated these children and let their spirits die, which would inevitably be followed by physical death. These families often did not have enough food, and these disabled children would never develop skills that would allow them to contribute to the family's welfare. That's just the way it was—there was no real sadness. And this horrifying policy wasn't unique to Korea. In China during this same period, healthy female infants were routinely drowned because parents felt that girls didn't have the physical strength to work long, hard hours farming rice.

Not long after my parents and I returned from the clinic, I began to feel that everyone around me was treating me as if I were meant to die. I could sense my mother's hesitancy toward me. For instance, she did not react as quickly to me as she did to my brother and sister. Emotionally she must have been torn, yet for a while I stopped trying to communicate my need for water or food, because I felt that this was how my mother wanted me to behave.

As the months passed, however, I realized that I had been handed a death warrant. Everyone around me—including my sister and brother, cousins, and neighbors—treated my impending death lightly, almost as if it were a matter of fact. When I finally figured out what was going on, I became determined to fight back.

Crying became my main form of communication. After all, if I didn't cry, I wouldn't get my fair share of food and water or get my diaper changed. Some days I howled. It wasn't long before my mother named me "the crying baby," and everyone else followed suit.

For the next three months I kept screaming until my mother routinely placed a bowl of rice in front of me. My hand-eye coordination was still very impaired, and it would take me 15 minutes to empty that bowl. If I got a half-dozen spoonfuls in my mouth, I was lucky. The rest landed on the floor or in my lap, which only served to frustrate my mother further. Aside from my mother, others thought my struggle with my rice bowl was funny. But it wasn't funny to *me* . . . I was trying to eat to survive.

I went outside as much as possible because the exercise made me feel better. It was the only way I could express myself and experience something good. More than anything, I wanted to learn to walk like normal people. Many times my parents would discover I was gone and wonder why I had left. It never occurred to them that life in a dark corner of the house had begun to feel like a coffin.

Once outside, I resembled a newborn colt as I struggled to walk on wobbly legs, often stumbling and falling down. The pain of trying to stand and walk was practically unbearable. Irate bicyclists would swerve to avoid me, and drivers would blare their horns. It was a humiliating experience, but I was determined to succeed. No matter what, I had to keep trying. Living, no matter how much hardship I had to endure, was better than death.

When I entered elementary school, the kids laughed at me and treated me like the village idiot. It wasn't long before I became a toy to them. They gnawed on my spirit the way a dog chews on a bone, and they often played cruel tricks on me. A favorite was to light a wooden match and place it in my fingers. They would giggle as the flame crept up, eventually burning the tips of my fingers. The tragedy was that I couldn't figure out how to put the match out. It never occurred to me to either drop it or blow it out.

My mother's nickname followed me into the schoolyard, for the kids knew exactly who she was talking about when she would ask, "Where's my crying baby?"

I had other nicknames, such as "Ugly Boy." Some people thought that I looked like an animal and walked with an awkward movement that didn't seem human. My hair was always mussed up, and sometimes large patches were missing because my mother treated my head lice with a strong chemical that burned my skin and destroyed my hair follicles. My mouth was twisted, and one eye was bigger and lower than the other. Because I was constantly drooling, my mother gave me handkerchiefs to clean up the saliva. And my eyes ran incessantly.

I hated being called "Ugly Boy." But I hated even more the day my brother said, in front of the neighborhood kids, "You were supposed to die a long time ago so that I could get your rice." I suffered tremendous hurt that day. If I couldn't trust *him,* then I had no one.

I was terribly envious of the other kids who had friends, and I longed for a playmate who would care about me. I didn't want to be popular—I only wanted one friend. Eventually I became so desperate that I was willing to do whatever it took.

One afternoon an older boy promised me that he would be my friend if the following morning I would bring him some watermelon and rice cakes. I was beyond joy; I was ecstatic. Later, I ran into the house beaming with an ear-to-ear grin. No one could figure out what was going on with me, especially my mother. Strangely, my happiness seemed to worry everyone, but I offered them no information.

That night after everyone was asleep, I quietly crawled to the opposite side of the room where my parents were sleeping and stole some money from my father's pants. The next eight hours were the longest of my life. I couldn't sleep because I knew that when the sun came up I was finally going to have a friend.

At the crack of dawn I was dressed and eating breakfast, with the money I'd stolen from my father hidden in my shoe. My mother entered the kitchen and stood with a confused look on her face as she watched me wolf down my food and charge out the back door.

Ten minutes later, I was sitting in front of the doorway of a local market when the owner arrived to open up. I entered and went straight to the crate of watermelons. I carefully examined every melon, set on purchasing the best one. I finally picked one out, paid for it (along with a premium for fresh-baked rice cakes), and watched the grocer pack up what to me was a pot of gold.

This older kid had asked me to meet him in an alley. I was there an hour early, cradling my king's ransom in the paper sack. When he arrived with five of his friends, I was so overjoyed that I hurried toward them, holding the bag out. In the process, I stumbled, and the bag fell to the ground. The watermelon rolled out and broke open. Immediately the kid and his friends began yelling.

"You dumb idiot!"

"What the heck's the matter with you?"

"Look what you did, Ugly Boy!"

They scooped up the watermelon and rice cakes and ordered me to sit beside a filthy garbage can. I tried to stay calm and complied with their demand as if it were a routine punishment among friends. For several minutes I sat beside that garbage can and watched these kids enjoying the treats I had brought. They were laughing together and having a good time, and I honestly felt that I had kept my end of the bargain.

When they finished, I stood and walked over to them, expecting that the older kid would throw his arm around my shoulders and walk with me to school. Instead, he punched me solidly in the stomach. I dropped to my knees, then forced myself to get up—even as I fought to catch my breath. Because I believed that this older boy had finally accepted me as a friend, I thought that his hitting me was part of a game or something. Moments later, he and his friends began throwing the watermelon rinds at me, and a few even hurled dirt clods, one of which hit me squarely in the head. When the barrage finally stopped, I stood in front of these six kids with a pile of rinds scattered at my feet and dirt smeared on my swollen, tear-streaked face. They laughed and made faces at me until they grew bored and walked away. Having failed to buy a friend, I also felt remorseful about stealing from my father.

The real tragedy of this story is that at one point while I was standing before these kids suffering their abuse, I actually began laughing with them because I thought that after they laughed *at* me, they would laugh *with* me. But they never did. As I watched that group of kids walk away, I made up my mind that no matter how long it took, one day I was going to be normal like those boys. Over the next few months, however, I had no choice but to isolate myself from the neighborhood kids. I just couldn't stand any more pain.

A short distance from my house was the Golden River, which was a branch of the much larger Han River. I would go there every day after school and sit along the bank, trying to make sense of the world in which I lived such a painful and unrewarding existence. I felt there was a cruel injustice to it all.

My family was not particularly religious, even though my father was a Buddhist, and my mother a Catholic. Yet she would occasionally talk about Jesus and read to me from her Bible.

While sitting beside the river, I recalled returning home one afternoon in tears. I shouted angrily at my mother that I was furious with her God and everything He had created. She sat me down on the floor and wrapped her arms around me. After I stopped crying, she explained that God was not responsible for the mean-spirited attitudes of the neighborhood kids. Reading from her Bible, she pointed out that after God had created the heavens and the earth, He observed all of His creation and said that everything was good. God didn't say that *some* of what He created was good or that *the majority* of His creation was good. He said that *everything* was good. And so, according to my mother, if bad things had since come into being, God wasn't responsible, people were. While her words did little to ease my frustration over the childhood war zone that greeted me each morning when I stepped outside my front door, they did help quiet my anger toward God.

As the weeks passed, I began to focus on the good that God created. Sitting by the river, I was mesmerized by the colorful fish swimming peacefully in and around the tall grasses and moss-covered rocks, and by the sight and sound of the water flowing by. Everything in the river appeared balanced by a system of mutual need, support, and cooperation. I thought, *How lucky those fish are to have a place to come to every day. To have a place where they are needed and wanted. To have things to do and things to look forward to. How lucky they must be.*

If there was such a thing as a next life, I wanted to come back as one of those fish. They seemed to know so much that the neighborhood kids had missed. Why couldn't *we* get along like the fish in the river? Why did those kids keep picking on me? They knew who and what I was—it wasn't like I was trying to hide anything or that I was trying to be something I wasn't. I was willing to do anything to make myself a better person, so why wouldn't they give me a little more time? That was all I wanted—just a little more time. Was that asking too much?

As I stared down into the water, I noticed that a small group of fish had separated from the school and were gathered around an older fish that appeared to be sick or even dying. The sight brought to mind a lesson I had learned months earlier in school. The teacher had read from a book about birds, and this particular lesson was focused on geese. She told us that when these beautiful birds fly in formation, if one of them got sick, wounded, or shot, two geese would drop out of formation to help protect it. Even if the ailing bird fell to the ground, those two others would stay with it until it either died or was able to fly again, at which time they would launch into another formation to catch up with the flock.

I couldn't help but think how beautiful life would be if only we had as much sense as these wonderful birds and stood with each other during the difficult and bad times, instead of leaving those who need a little help to fend for themselves—or even worse, to treat them in such a way that makes life harder for them.

If God truly was loving, and all of His creation was "good," then perhaps it would be within the natural scheme of His universe to send someone to help me. The more I thought about the hopeless dilemma I awoke to each morning, the more I had to believe that some*how*, some*way*, some*where*, God would send some*one* to help me find a way out of my misery.

chapter 2 :::
Meeting Master Ko Soo

:::

Most of the neighborhood kids ran away from the middle-aged man known as Master Ko Soo, who had a mean-looking face and a scar across one cheek. While physically he was of average size, the way he carried himself suggested a man of great strength. He had thick hands, which often appeared swollen and banged up. And his cold, piercing eyes could cut straight through to a person's soul.

Master Ko was a shoemaker by trade. He would sit at his workbench in a corner of the small space he rented, tapping nails and gluing on new soles. He seemed to particularly enjoy polishing the leather, and had several rows of polishes and waxes neatly arranged in a nearby wooden rack. It was obvious that he took great pride in his work. At times he was even heard humming to himself.

Every day at 4 P.M., he would close his shop and walk eight blocks to his three-room house, which needed paint and had several cracked windows. After entering through the broken gate, he'd gaze at his small flower garden before leaping onto the porch and entering the house in one smooth motion.

Master Ko had never married and lived alone. As far as anyone knew, he was without family and seemed to prefer it that way. His only companion was a small pet monkey—at times he would fuss over the animal and become withdrawn when it was ill.

Unlike the other kids, I wasn't afraid of Master Ko. In a strange way, I felt drawn to him. I was about six years old when I began to spy on him, both at his shop (where I'd watch him through the window) and at his home. There was an alley that ran along one side of his house and a broken fence that I could easily climb over, so I used to sneak up to the house and peek through his window.

Master Ko's home was different from others in the neighborhood because his living room had no carpeting or furniture—it just consisted of a highly polished wooden floor. Beyond the living room was a small kitchen and bedroom.

Several days a week at 5 P.M., a group of Korean men would come to Master Ko's house. I watched them remove their street clothes and put on what looked like white pajamas. Their pants were pulled tight by a drawstring, while their top tunics folded like a double-breasted suit coat. Each man tied a cloth belt around his waist, leaving the two ends of the belt hanging loosely in front. Everyone wore either white or red belts, which looked new compared to Master Ko's frayed black belt.

After a while I figured out that the master's living room was actually a classroom setting, and the men who came to his house were his students. Whatever it was that he was teaching them was a mystery to me. I could see them kick their legs and arms in the air and move around the floor in strange-looking stances—it didn't look as if they were dancing, nor was it like any game played by the neighborhood kids. Then one afternoon, I saw Master Ko pair off his students, and I could plainly see that what these men were practicing were blocks, kicks, and punches that made up some kind of fighting art.

As the weeks passed, I became fascinated with what I later learned was the Korean martial art of Tang Soo Do. The speed and power of these men was astonishing and sometimes scary. They moved with incredible precision and split-second timing. Their coordination and physical skills seemed supernatural to me because I was so awkward and clumsy. It dawned on me that if I could somehow learn to move like these men, I would make the neighborhood kids look stupid. Maybe this was a way for all of us to come together on a level playing field. Was Master Ko my long-awaited godsend?

A week later I summoned up the courage to stand on the master's front porch and knock on the door. I held my breath as the sound of footsteps fast approached on the other side. An instant later the door swung open, and Master Ko stood in front of me. I had never been this close to him before, and now he looked like a monster. He seemed to have an unseen energy that pushed my body backwards.

"What do you want?" he inquired in an unfriendly voice.

My eyes were drawn to the group of students behind him. Their kicks were so fast and powerful that the rice cloth of their pants cracked in the air like a bullwhip.

"It's cold out here," I replied, not knowing what else to say.

His face remained expressionless. "Very observant. Was there something else? I'm busy."

I hesitated, and he started to close the door. I pushed my hand out to stop it from closing. Master Ko's eyes widened and his nostrils flared. I couldn't believe I had done that.

"I was wondering . . . ," I began, and then choked up again.

The master's chest swelled. "You can wonder by yourself! You don't need me for that!" he shouted angrily.

"No, wait!" I quickly wiped my mouth and eyes with my handkerchief. My heart was racing as I practically spit out, "Could I come in and watch?"

Master Ko glanced over his shoulder at his students, then swung the door open. "All right," he said impatiently. "You can watch, but that's all. Sit over there in that corner and don't say a word."

"Okay," I said. I stepped inside on unsteady legs.

His hand hit my shoulder like an artillery shell. "Not 'okay'! The correct reply is 'Yes, sir!'"

"Yes, sir!" I cried out.

"If you don't learn anything else in this room, learn the meaning of respect and obedience—or go home!"

"Yes, sir!"

I made my way to a corner of the room, where I sat and watched in silence. What I saw inside that room was awesome. Whenever Master Ko moved, the walls and floor shook as if rocked by thunder. His lightning-fast punches and kicks whizzed past the faces of his students and made their hair stand up in the breeze. His jump kicks were so graceful that he seemed to possess a natural flying ability. And when he shouted in unison with his strikes, the noise hurt my ears.

Physical injuries were common in the class, and Master Ko often meted out punishment. I watched him repeatedly correct a mistake that was being made by one of his students. At the time, it didn't seem to me like an important error. But apparently this student did something to aggravate the master, who came after him with kicks and punches. The student ran backwards with a terrified look in his eyes—and moments later dropped to the floor, half-senseless. Without hesitation, Master Ko grabbed the shoulder of the student's uniform, yanked him to his feet, and then shouted to the class, "Attention!"

Everyone scrambled to line up. Master Ko stood before them like a one-man firing squad. He was livid. "I am like a swordmaker who is handed a piece of raw metal!" he exclaimed. "I place this metal into the fire, and when it becomes red-hot, I pound it with all my strength and will, continually moving it back and forth between the fire and my anvil until my work is completed! My sole purpose is to make the best sword possible, which may take years, if not an entire lifetime! But I will not accept from this metal anything less than the strongest and mightiest sword that it can be! Do you understand that?"

"Yes, sir!" the entire class shouted.

"I will not tolerate mistakes! In this room you are to strive for absolute perfection! You are to listen, obey, and follow my instructions 100 percent!"

"Yes, sir!" the men shouted again.

I sat in the corner of Master Ko's studio and watched in silence for three long months. One evening after the students had left, I stood inside the front door, waiting to be acknowledged.

Master Ko finally walked over to me. "Are you wondering again?" he asked bluntly.

"Not exactly—sir."

"Wondering is for deep thinkers, but in a battle for your life, wondering will get you killed."

"Yes, sir."

"Say what is on your mind."

I looked up at him and worried that he might see me as Ugly Boy. I didn't want that. I needed for him to feel differently about me. "Can I train here? With the others?" I asked, making a point not to take my eyes off his.

He peered down at me for a long time, and it felt as if he were looking deep inside of me. "You're the one they call the crying baby," he finally said in a matter-of-fact tone.

"Yes, sir," I replied while lowering my eyes to the floor.

"Look at me!" he roared, sending a shock wave through my body.

"Yes, sir!"

"Why do they call you that? What are you crying about?"

"Different things. Sir! I guess I'm not like the others, and it makes me sad."

"What's wrong with you?"

It occurred to me that this man knew a lot about me, probably from talking to the people whose shoes he repaired. "Everyone says I'm clumsy," I answered. "And some say I'm stupid."

"I didn't ask you what others say. I asked what was wrong with you—not them."

"Well, I guess . . . to me . . . I'm not as bad as everyone says."

"There is no such thing as bad," he replied, keeping his eyes on me. "Only good, better, and best. Which do you want to be?"

He had asked a difficult question that I had never thought about before. Finally, I told him the truth: "I just want to be like you, sir."

"I see. And you think that training here will allow you to accomplish that?"

"Yes, sir."

"I know that your family has little money, and none of my students train for free."

"I could pay whatever you ask."

"I have heard it said that you steal. I will not allow that. Not here!"

"Yes, sir," I replied. I wasn't about to challenge him regarding this allegation.

"You can earn your lessons by cleaning the school and running errands for me. Return tomorrow and tell me if your father is agreeable to that arrangement."

"Yes, sir!"

"And one other thing: Never again in my presence are you to use the word *bad* to describe yourself. There is nothing wrong with you!"

"Yes, sir!"

I was filled with joy, and for the first time in my life I didn't feel like a weakling. I ran all the way home, jumping obstacles like a gazelle. I no longer felt clumsy, even though I still was.

I was overjoyed when my parents agreed to Master Ko's offer. Besides allowing me to clean up the school, my father offered to give Master Ko a five-pound sack of rice every month. And my mother was grateful that I had a place to go—at the very least, I wasn't returning home every day with torn and dirty clothes, battle-scarred from being beaten up by the neighborhood kids.

The next day I returned to Master Ko's studio and after class told him the good news.

For three more months, all I did was clean the school, run errands for the master, and silently observe class. Cleaning the studio made me so happy, even though it took two hours to do so. When I finished, Master Ko would carefully inspect the floor, and if he didn't see himself reflected in the wood, he made me scrub and polish it all over again. Every time I missed a spot, he yelled at me. This treatment was much different from what I had experienced at school and at home, where even if I did something poorly, I was told that I did a good job. Except for Master Ko, everyone made excuses for my disabilities and shortcomings, and in so doing caused my self-confidence and self-esteem to fall. When Master Ko refused to settle for anything short of perfection, I knew that it was the only way I could ever begin to feel normal. Someone had to raise the bar, and Master Ko did just that.

One day Master Ko took his students on a field trip. We followed the path of a river that led to the ocean. It was the first time I'd seen the ocean, and I was amazed at how the bottom of the sky seemed to join with the far end of the water.

I spotted a group of fishermen catching fish. One of them reeled in a large perch, and I was impressed by its size.

The master came over to me and asked, "You think that fish is big?"

"Yes, sir!"

"You know, some fishes are much bigger than you."

"Really?" I replied with surprise.

"Yes."

"How big?"

"As big as a small house," Master Ko replied.

"A fish that big? What's it called?"

"It's called a 'whale.'"

"Wow! Can I see one?"

"It is rare that anyone sees a whale."

As I again pondered the vast horizon, I thought about this massive fish the master talked about. "Sir, who lives at the end of the ocean?" I asked.

"It is a place called 'America,' and the people who live there are called 'Americans.' They are big and tall, and they eat very well and live in big houses."

"Sir, I want to go there," I said enthusiastically.

The master looked at me closely. "You will have to grow to be a strong swimmer," he said. "A little fish cannot make it across the ocean."

"One day I will be as strong as a whale," I said confidently. "And then I will swim to America."

"I believe you will, son. One day, I believe you will."

That was my first inkling of wanting to go to America. I was only six years old.

I felt safe whenever I was inside Master Ko's studio. I had so many problems as a child—physically, mentally, emotionally, and spiritually—but they all vanished the moment I walked into his school and he handed me my mops, pails, brushes, and polishing cloths. What a joy it was to finally have a place to go where I had a purpose and felt accepted, just like the fish in the Golden River. Although I still was not being taught the physical moves of Master Ko's martial art, the fact that I was a part of his world gave me the confidence to star standing up for myself.

There was a particular kid in school who went out of his way to humiliate me in front of the other children. Every day, he would make a point of finding me—when he did, he would mock me, make jokes about me, and punch me in the stomach. I did all I could to avoid this kid, including constantly changing my route to and from school. Then one day I had finally had enough. Instead of waiting for him to find me, *I* sought *him* out. I walked up to him and said that I wanted to hear his latest joke about me. I also told him to punch me in the stomach as hard as he could. The kid was furious, and really wailed away on me. This time he didn't punch me once in the stomach; instead, he pummeled me in the face and body repeatedly. By the time he was finished, I was barely able to struggle back to my feet. But I was determined to take everything he could dish out and still be standing when he walked away.

The next day the kid was shocked when I appeared before him again. I was all banged up, and one eye was swollen shut. As I had done before, I held both hands at my sides and told him that I wasn't afraid of him, so he should go ahead and beat me up. Once again I took a horrible beating, but I managed to get to my feet as the kid walked away with his friends. Much to this bully's amazement, I repeated this routine for an entire week. Every day he came to school, I'd find him and tell him to give me his best punch. After a while he began avoiding me, and soon *he* actually became afraid of *me*. In the end, I was victorious through nonviolence. Because he knew that I had taken away his ability to instill fear in me, I became a strong opponent. I have since learned that this is something bullies always avoid.

Although Master Ko didn't speak much and rarely displayed his soft side, I felt that he did care about me. Like the geese that leave the flock to protect and nurture a sick or wounded bird, I believe that Master Ko sensed that I was a troubled and lost child who needed help. I think he responded to my plea because he could see that I wasn't a quitter. He observed me watching class in silence for three months and then cleaning the school every day for another three months. I always came prepared to work, and I was never late. There were two things Master Ko couldn't tolerate—one was a quitter, and the other was a loser. And he often said that a loser was simply a person who quit.

It wasn't long before I began to idolize Master Ko. I wanted to look, walk, and dress like him. His every wish, both expressed and anticipated, was my command. It wasn't long before idolatry turned to worship, and I began to expect Master Ko to be everything to me. This didn't sit well with the master, who one day sat me down and gave me a stern lecture.

"I am not your friend," he explained. "And don't expect me to clean up after you, because I am not your mother. Most of all, I am not your father. I am not someone you bring all your problems to. I am not here to pat you on your shoulder and tell you that everything is going to be all right. Don't expect me to listen to everything you have to say and agree with you, because this is not going to happen. I am simply your master— nothing more, nothing less. Every time you see me, I want you to think *Yes, sir!, No, sir!,* and *Attention!* If I ask you to do things, you are to do exactly what I ask. If you don't, you are going to be punished."

He paused at the sight of the tears forming in my eyes. I was crushed. Master Ko had become a father figure to me, and I couldn't understand why he was so against that relationship. To me it seemed harmless and subtle, but to him it spelled disaster.

"There are only 24 hours in a day," he continued. "You need to spend some of that time with your mother and your father. You also have to spend time with your friends. If the day comes that *I* am your mother and your father, then on that day you will not take time to talk to either of them. And soon you will stop seeing them. There is an important difference between your father and me: I am your teacher and guide; I am not someone you can lean on. That is what your father is for—for you to lean on and cry to and talk about unnecessary things. My purpose is to teach you perfection, to put you on a path to excellence and keep you there. There is no room for error with me, not so much as an inch. But there *is* room for error with your father—he will allow that. But I will not."

I have since learned that Master Ko was right. The relationships I shared with my father, mother, and master were all basically different. Today, my father and I relate on a physical and mental level, while the bond I share with my mother is emotional in nature. Neither of these two relationships demand, seek, or require perfection. Only the relationship I had with Master Ko was one whose sole purpose was the achievement of absolute perfection. Because of this, my relationship with my master was always a spiritual one. Throughout my life, Master Ko is the only person who demanded, and sought to instill, perfection in me, which he felt was his duty in life as my teacher and guide. Although he was a shoemaker by profession, the martial arts were his life and the source of his spirituality.

My master often said that along my journey to perfection I would encounter many setbacks and disappointments, but I should remain diligent. Few people in life truly seek perfection, and far fewer take on the role of teacher and guide. These people belong to a very exclusive club, and they are to a large extent destined to be forever alienated from the masses.

When I reflect upon the early decisions that set me on this path with my master, I know that from the outset I had the capability of making the right choices. Accepting the master's statement that there was nothing wrong with me was the beginning of the end of my physical and mental disabilities.

chapter 3 :::
Conquering My Disabilities

:::

To a large degree, I attribute my ability to overcome my disabilities to my training in the martial arts. Prior to beginning my actual lessons, I was greatly helped by Master Ko's insistence that I sit quietly and center my attention on the classes taking place out on the training floor. In addition, my regular cleaning of the school, together with the master's constant demand for perfection, gave me the ability to complete even the simplest of tasks.

It is true that I arrived in this world damaged in the shipping. As I touched on previously, by the time I was three years old, my parents recognized that there was something lacking in my ability to mentally process information. Something in my brain was short-circuiting, and whatever it was also made it impossible for me to stand still. If I didn't constantly monitor my balance and adjust it, I would keel over. It was akin to being a tightrope walker, where if I stopped and stood still for even a few seconds, I would fall. My

need to continually readjust my balance was a major problem for me—
yet, much to everyone's amazement, Master Ko got me to stand still after
only a few lessons.

When I began my actual instruction, the first thing the master taught me
was the horse stance, which is the basic training position of the martial arts.
This stance gets its name because if the student is viewed head-on, he or she
appears to be sitting in a saddle. Both legs are apart, knees are bent and forced
out, and the buttocks are tucked forward so that his or her center of gravity
falls directly over the tailbone. While the person does appear to be riding a
horse, this stance actually came from early martial artists observing bears.
In the entire animal kingdom, few animals are as well balanced on two legs
as a bear. Its legs are bent, paws slightly turned in, back straight, with its
center directly over its tailbone.

It was this basic stance that enabled me to finally establish a communication between my body and the ground. Somehow, learning this
position turned on a switch inside me that, for whatever reason, had previously been in the off position. No longer did I continually sway; no
longer did I fall down while trying to walk or run. Now that I had a solid
base, Master Ko began to teach me particular movements that gave me
coordination and physical strength. Most important, he instilled a sense
of timing in me.

When I entered first grade at the age of seven, my biggest problem
was this very lack of timing. I just couldn't connect my physical and mental worlds in a proper fashion. Whenever the teacher would ask me a question, I would know the answer but couldn't say it fast enough. Although
I knew the words, I couldn't get them to come out of my mouth.

I have since learned that this is a common problem for patients recov-
ering from strokes. When they are asked their first names, they instantly
know it in their minds, but they can't speak it. If you say their names for
them, they will nod their heads up and down. As a result of having a stroke,
something in the patients' brains has become short-circuited.

This was my experience in the classroom. Long after the teacher had
moved on to the next subject, I would raise my hand and, upon being
acknowledged, blurt out the answer to what I had been asked five minutes before. The other students would giggle, but I didn't care. I had the
right answer, even if I came up with it a few minutes late.

However, after I'd spent many hours joining speed with accuracy, the "mental lag" that had plagued me since childhood gradually disappeared. During sparring, my timing had to be fixed or I would be continually hit by my opponent. This was one of many survival switches that were switched from the "off" to the "on" position over time.

But I had several other problems. I couldn't talk well, and my strange-sounding enunciation often drew either laughter or confused looks. My reading and writing abilities were below standard, and I always needed extra tutoring. Note-taking was by far the most difficult task for me at school.

Even though many of my classmates kept on making fun of me and physically abusing me outside of class, I always wanted to come to school. I would sit in front of the classroom and was never a disciplinary problem, especially since Master Ko had taught me obedience and responsibility. So no matter how sick I was, I always insisted on going to school. As the master had told me, I really needed to be with my peers. No matter how hard they were on me, I knew that they were important to my getting better. My life wasn't going to improve by sitting in the corner at home.

If I were to name one aspect of the martial arts that I feel was responsible for my overcoming my mental and physical disabilities, it would be the years of practicing the physical animal movements. Earlier, I mentioned the horse stance, which was derived from observing bears in the wild. Practically all of martial arts' basic movements and body weapons are the result of observing the fighting tactics of a wide range of animals.

Thousands of years ago, early founders of the Korean and Japanese martial arts structured their basic movements and stances after observing such animals as tigers, horses, monkeys, lions, elephants, and bears, to name but a few. These animals were born knowing their movements—they didn't have to go to school to learn how to defend themselves. For example, from birth the boa constrictor instinctively knows how to wrap its coils around its prey. A young tiger doesn't have to be taught how to deliver a claw to the eyes of an attacker. And horses are born with incredible kicking abilities. All members of the animal kingdom are born with a knowledge of self-defense, and each has its own unique system with all its switches in the "on" position.

Master Ko taught his students that in the beginning humans were born with a similar survival system of self-defense in place. Long before we ever became civilized, the need to survive was paramount. Like many animals below us on the evolutionary chain, humans were born with: (1) a keen sense of our surroundings and the ability to instantly detect danger; (2) an understanding of the rhythm of life; (3) the coordination through which we could deliver our movements with great accuracy; and (4) natural physical strength. Those who didn't possess all four of these qualities were protected by someone who did or they simply perished.

Master Ko explained that the cause of my childhood disabilities was the result of humans becoming civilized. After many hundreds of years, most people no longer made their daily physical survival a top priority. Instead, this job was handed over to our protectors—mainly the police and military. Thus, humans' inborn system of self-defense was gradually disarmed, causing many of its circuit breakers to switch to their "off" positions.

Even though I was having extreme difficulty communicating with my environment and within myself, the good news was that all my hard wiring was still intact. All I needed to do was find a way to activate the connections. While my years of martial arts training were what turned on so many of these dormant switches, I believe that other endeavors in life may have accomplished the same result.

As my training progressed and I gradually overcame my disabilities, the workouts became increasingly more strenuous. Master Ko always pushed his students to the limit and often said, "You must learn self-control, self-discipline, and the ability to concentrate. If you can't learn how to concentrate and focus, then I can't do much."

For the master, speed was developed through physical conditioning that included strength, endurance, and flexibility exercises. He honed and hardened our bodies through training regimes that drove us to sheer exhaustion. The key was practice, practice, practice. (Today I tell my students that my first name is Practice, my middle name is Practice, and my last name is Practice.)

What really helped me to recover from my physical disabilities, especially my overall uncoordinated movements, was the continual rep-etition. Hundreds of hours spent repeating the same exact move over and over helped immensely to establish the neuromuscular pathways that, prior to training, simply were not functioning properly for me. Besides the grueling hours of daily repetition practiced in class, in the winters we regularly submerged our bodies into ice ponds, and in the summer we ran ten miles beneath the scorching sun.

Master Ko frequently said, "When you make mistakes, I am going to be there to correct you with mother love," which was a bamboo stick that he would crack across our legs, butts, and upper bodies.

There were a total of 24 bamboo sticks of assorted sizes and shapes hanging on a wall of our studio. Each had a name: master love, mother love, sister love, father love, and so forth. The hardest stick was master love, because it came from the section closest to the bamboo root, so its center was solid. Master love was used primarily for punishment. The next hardest, and most commonly used, was mother love (the center of this section of bamboo was hollow and slightly pliable). Mother love got its name from the caring, nurturing, and sacrifice of our mothers. And so when a student received mother love, it was in the spirit of the unselfish caring, nurturing, and sacrifice extended to us by the master.

Many Americans view the striking of students with bamboo sticks as abuse. But to Koreans practicing martial arts in those days, "mother love" was the medicine that not only taught us discipline and respect, but hardened our bodies. After three months of receiving my share of mother love, the rocks that the neighbor kids threw at me felt like marshmallows; after six months, the rocks never hit me; and after a year, the kids stopped throwing them altogether.

Students who practice the Korean martial arts are famous for their ability to execute high kicks. Not surprisingly, Master Ko placed a supreme value on his students' ability to jump. A particularly effective kick we used was called the eagle kick. Technically, the eagle does not kick; rather, it swoops down on its prey and grabs it with its talons. So in a sense this highly skilled bird is performing a flying kick, which it executes in a power-dive against fleeing prey. Clearly, this is a move that requires precise timing and accuracy. These are the qualities Master Ko wanted us to demonstrate when performing the eagle kick.

Our training in jumping was intense. Often in the early morning hours we would meet in the cornfields, where we would spend hours jumping over varying heights of corn. When we missed and damaged the stalk, Master Ko would be right there to give us mother love. Eventually I was able to jump once in the air and deliver six kicks to my opponent's head and body before landing on my feet. During exhibitions I routinely jumped over 16 people before breaking three stacks of boards positioned at the other end. Of course this took extreme concentration and required split-second precision of both speed and timing. At the height of my world exhibition tour, I was so proficient at aerial kicking that the distances achieved in both my standing and running jump kicks approached track-and-field world records in the high jump and long jump.

When I look back at my early years of training from ages 6 to 15, I remember that they were oftentimes brutal. Yet I know today that had my training not been that tough—if the master had not given me mother love and physically rode roughshod over me, I don't feel that I would ever have stood up for myself; consequently, I wouldn't be here today to share these things with you. Yes, it was difficult, and even today I can recall the physical pain. But I just kept thinking about those kids in my neighborhood, silently telling them, "If you laugh at me, hopefully the day will come when I can laugh with you, because deep inside I know I am equal to you." I wasn't embarrassed by their ridicule, because in my eyes I was already at the bottom and couldn't sink any lower. I tried not to spend time worrying about how the kids treated me, since I knew that the only way I could go was up. There were moments, however, when my failure to keep up with the others did depress me.

Several times a year Master Ko would test students for promotion. Whenever testing came up, I was either not included on the list, or if I tested, I failed. The following day I always stood in class and watched many of the other students being promoted, which was denoted by adding a stripe to their white belt or by receiving a new belt that was entirely a solid color. This went on for more than a year. Then one night after class, I found myself at home sitting alone in the corner, still wearing my uniform and looking down at my belt, which I had untied and held in my hands. It was still solid white—not one single stripe on it. An entire year of training had not resulted in a single promotion.

After a while it occurred to me that I didn't have to put myself in a position of being in competition with the other students. *I* was the only one who really mattered. In the months that followed, I began to ask myself, *How are you doing today compared to how you were doing yesterday?* This approach worked well for me. Even if I made the smallest degree of progress, I felt that I'd had a good week.

One night after a particularly difficult week of training, I was at home, again contemplating my stripeless white belt when I realized that I could establish a second promotional yardstick. In addition to Master Ko's promotions, I could promote myself at such time when I felt that I had achieved my next level of proficiency. The more I thought about it, the better the idea sounded. After all, I was a retarded kid and Ugly Boy, so there should be an exception made for the deck being stacked against me. Using a pencil, I made a tiny hash mark on one edge of my belt that represented a single stripe to me. The mark was barely visible, and I thought that only I would be aware of it. I went to bed that night feeling quite proud.

When the next group of students was promoted, and they were celebrating among themselves, I walked away and sat in a corner of the school, admiring the tiny hash mark that I had made on my belt several months earlier. Unfortunately, the master noticed this. That night he asked me to stay after class. He was highly displeased, and he gave me a strong dose of mother love. "There's no honor in self-promoting!" he yelled over and over as he whacked me with the bamboo stick.

Years later I came to see the wisdom of this. In any martial arts school there can be only one promotional gradient—that of the master, who has absolute power and authority. If it were any other way, that particular martial art would lose its honor. To promote oneself outside the master's wishes is demeaning to all the other students, but most important, to the master himself. It was one of many lessons along my journey that I had to learn the hard way.

Over the next four years I painstakingly continued with my training. Compared to the other students' levels of advancement, I was like the fabled tortoise to the hare. But I refused to quit. Month after month, year after year, I worked my way through the ranks one stripe and belt at a time. Then, shortly after my tenth birthday, I was awarded my black belt. All my family and friends and schoolteachers attended the ceremony. It was the proudest day of my life. Because in the martial arts a child can't be viewed as a full black belt until reaching the age of 16, mine was an "honorary" black belt. This didn't matter to me, because I had satisfactorily learned the required curriculum. The fact that my belt was considered honorary was only a technicality.

A week after being awarded my black belt, I waited for the other students to leave and then quietly approached Master Ko, who was sitting at a small table that he liked to call his office.

"Excuse me, sir," I said after clearing the frog from my throat.

"Yes?" he replied in his usual expressionless monotone.

"I just wanted to thank you for all that you've done for me. I know it hasn't been easy for you, and I have been a very hard student to teach. Much of the time I have had two left feet and always seemed to take forever to get it right. I think I have taken more mother love than anyone here. Even with my cleaning the school for you, I often felt that it probably wasn't worth all the extra attention you have had to give me."

"I am a teacher, son. Not all students are the same," he said.

"Yes, I know. But I wanted to point something out that means a lot to me. I was thinking maybe it would help." I paused, waiting to see if I were overstepping my bounds.

"Yes?"

"Well, when I first came here, there were many students who were a lot better than me. That's not saying much, I know. But these guys really seemed like they had everything working in their favor. Over the years I watched them receive one promotion after the next, while I stayed a white belt. Some of them even made their red belt, which was something I only dreamed about. Many times they waved their belts in my face, but I refused to quit. Anyway, now that I'm a black belt, I suddenly realized that these guys aren't here anymore. They quit, but I'm still here. And now I'm a higher rank than they were when they left. It just took me a whole lot longer. I guess what I want you to know is that I appreciate all you have put up with in my training, and I'm going to stay here as long as you'll continue to want to train me—sir."

It was the first and only time I saw Master Ko in a state of speechlessness. After a while, a hint of tears welled up in his eyes, and he said, "Son, I will never forget what you just said to me."

A week later while teaching class, he suddenly roared to the students, "A black belt is simply a white belt who never quit! Do not forget that!" And he glanced in my direction and offered a subtle grin, which was rare for Master Ko Soo.

chapter 4 :::
Child Soldier in the Korean War

•••
•••

For the first ten years of my life, my family had not known a day when the Japanese didn't occupy our homeland. We suffered extreme hardship, as there was little work and constant food shortages. For the most part, the Japanese had broken the spirit of the Korean people.

On August 6, 1945, the United States dropped an atomic bomb on Hiroshima, and three days later, they dropped one on Nagasaki. Radio reports at the time said that the catastrophic devastation had put the fear of God into the Japanese. Soon after, news began swirling around our village of Ansung that 120,000 Soviet troops had invaded Manchuria and the northern part of Korea. Although no one in our village knew why the Russians had done this, we assumed that they had not stormed into Korea to fight Koreans. The thought of their lining up the Japanese in their gun sights gave us hope.

Hours after Hiroshima had been leveled, the Kempeitai, or Japanese military police, in Ansung rounded up Koreans they knew were sympathetic to the revolutionary movement based in Manchuria. These people were dragged into the police station and brutally tortured for hours. The Japanese desperately wanted to know what was going on and were willing to execute on the spot anyone they felt was holding back information.

The Kempeitai tortured prisoners as readily and as brutally as Nazi Germany's gestapo had done. Savage beatings were routine, as were cold-blooded murders. Desperate screams were heard coming from the police station at all hours of the day and night. Because my father's brother was a key figure in the revolutionary movement, our family kept a close watch on that police station.

Two days after the Soviet invasion, I awoke in the early morning and immediately sensed that something was different. Normally the Japanese were patrolling the streets at sunrise, blaring orders through their bullhorns. Their continual barrage of loud demands—everything from traffic detours to orders for us to come outside and bow to huge placards of their celebrated emperor—overpowered the senses. However, on this particular morning, everything outside was quiet. Moments later I could hear people in the street shouting, "The Japanese are gone! The Japanese are gone!"

I couldn't believe it. The news, if true, would be nothing short of a miracle. Even though I was only ten, I joined a large group of people to converge on the police station. Once inside, we stood in shock. The Japanese had left in a hurry, leaving everything behind. We walked through the station and spit on the walls. I even stole a pencil from one of the desks, because it made me feel good to know that I could walk into what was known as a Japanese chamber of horrors, take something, and walk out unchallenged. In a strange way, I felt as many of the others did—that I was having the last laugh.

Finally, we Koreans were living in our own country. Over the next two weeks we defiantly tore down all remnants of the Japanese: road signs, statues, billboards, pictures, photographs, and official proclamations—everything! On September 2, 1945, the United States accepted the Japanese surrender, which was cause for great celebration.

After the Japanese were thrown out of Korea, it took a long time to restore the country to order. Gangsters and American soldiers who remained in Seoul fought constantly in the streets. Meanwhile, far away, the political heads of the two large superpowers of the United States and the Soviet Union were trying to figure out just who was going to govern our newly emancipated country. For decades the Japanese had told the world that the Korean people were dumb and uneducated, and now they were telling both Soviet and American leaders that there was no one in Korea who was intelligent enough to run the country. According to the Japanese, Koreans had a herd mentality: A slave was always a slave, and therefore it would take 50 to 100 years to reeducate Korea in order to produce its own leader. This was the Japanese prediction, and the Soviet and American leaders believed it. As a temporary solution, the United States and the USSR agreed to divide the country in half at the 38th parallel. Later they would focus on bringing the two halves together into a single, unified Korea.

Because there was no one in Korea who was qualified to run the country, the United States leaders proposed that Syngman Rhee, a Korean who lived in the U.S. and had been educated there, be considered for the position. Subsequently, Rhee was flown to Korea and became the first President of South Korea by popular elections held in May 1948. With the support of the United States, President Rhee organized a temporary government to oversee South Korea, called the Republic of Korea (ROK), in August 1948. The northern half, or Democratic People's Republic of Korea (DPRK), would be overseen by the Russians, who expressed what appeared to everyone as a sincere willingness to help. While such an arrangement appeared sound in principle and even on paper, the faint beating of war drums could be heard coming from the north.

In February 1948, six months before Syngman Rhee took control of South Korea, his Russian-appointed counterpart, Kim Il Sung, who had lived in Russia and had been educated there, officially activated the Korean People's Army. In contrast to the South Korean military, North Korea's army was a commendable force. Then, a mere three weeks after President Rhee took office, Kim Il Sung, speaking as the head of the DPRK, boldly claimed jurisdiction over *all* Korea.

June 25, 1950 seemed like every other day in Ansung. I was 15 years old and was getting ready for dinner, when suddenly everyone in our house became aware of a popping sound. At first we thought that a neighbor was popping beans, which is the Korean version of popcorn. While the noise didn't get any louder, it didn't let up either. Minutes later, our curiosity got the best of us, and we walked outside. Along both sides of the street many of our neighbors stood outside their homes, focusing their attention on this same sound that clearly was coming from the north. No one seemed particularly concerned about it. Only later would we learn that this strange noise was actually a long and intensive volley of artillery and mortar fire emanating from the North Korean army.

The next morning, my siblings and I were anxiously awakened by our mother, who told us to quickly pack our things. Hours earlier and without warning, seven assault divisions of the North Korean army, which amounted to 90,000 soldiers, smashed headlong into totally unprepared units of South Korea's army. The assault was led by 150 tanks, and closely supported by 1,700 howitzers and self-propelled 76mm guns. And more than 200 Soviet-supplied aircraft gave them total domination of the skies.

The South Korean army had eight divisions, but only four were deployed along the 38th parallel. Far worse, the South Korean army had no air force, no heavy mortars, no medium artillery, and only relatively ineffective 2.36-inch rocket launchers. The North Koreans had T34 tanks—arguably the best tanks developed in WWII—and they advanced in a line formation, crushing beneath their steel treads hundreds of South Korean soldiers who tried desperately to stop them with powder charges and hand grenades. Unscathed, the tanks then began to roll through the frantic survivors as though they weren't even there.

Ansung was approximately 30 miles south of Seoul. We all knew that the soldiers would get to us slowly because of the rough mountain roads, but we knew they were coming. My father had gone in hopes of finding a safe haven to the south; my brothers, sisters, and I followed with my mother, who had given birth to twins two months before.

When we left, the main roads leading south were congested with more than 30,000 fleeing refugees. My mother tied a rope around my wrist, which she then attached to my older brother and sister. If we became separated, we would have been instantly lost in the surging crowd, if not trampled beneath its feet. It was tragic how the gut-wrenching panic that engulfed these thousands of frightened Koreans was much worse than what they had experienced during the Japanese occupation.

The following day we heard about the first of many atrocities that would follow in the next three years. You see, to move south from the capitol of Seoul, refugees and soldiers had to cross one of three bridges that spanned the Han River. With all three lanes of one of the bridges packed with a slow-moving mass of people, a demolition team under orders from the South Korean army blew up the bridge, sending more than 1,000 screaming victims plunging to their deaths. On top of that, exploding the bridge was supposed to stop the North Korean soldiers and their tanks at the Han River—yet most of the South Korean army's best, along with their equipment, were left trapped on the north side of the river. Within three days, Seoul fell into the hands of the North Korean army; over the next three years, Seoul would exchange hands five times.

My family and I kept moving south, one painful step at a time. There was little food or water, and many of the elderly who died were simply placed on the side of the road. The smell of human waste and decaying flesh began to permeate the air. Hardly anyone talked, because to do so wasted much-needed energy. The only sounds were those of the creaking oxcart wheels, the crying of the children, and the wailing of the infirm and unstable who were slowly losing their minds.

About 30 miles south of Ch'onan, we arrived at a military checkpoint, and I had to say good-bye to my brother, Duk, because every male child above the age of 12 was eligible to be drafted into the South Korean Army—on sight. (In the first month following the initial attack, 50,000 young men were inducted; by the end of 1950, the number had increased to 250,000!) At age 19, Duk was unquestionably old and strong enough. But that didn't ease our pain. Our family hugged him and shared our tears, and promised that we would all meet up again after this terrible war had ended.

Moments later I watched my brother being ushered off to an awaiting troop transport truck. Although I had escaped being drafted at several checkpoints (probably because I simply didn't look like soldier material), I was eventually chosen. After saying farewell to my mother and remaining siblings, I was hastily moved toward an identical troop transport truck that had days earlier taken my brother to the battlefront. I was scared to death.

Initially I was not eager to become part of the South Korean army and fight an enemy that was described to me only as "Communist soldiers." Because I had lived in occupied Korea for the majority of my life, I had only a vague sense of patriotism. My family had a Korean flag, but we were never allowed to display it. Moreover, having lived in a small village and possessing only a limited education, I had no understanding of world politics or why the North had attacked the South. All I knew was what I had been told in school for a year prior to the attack—that North Koreans were different from South Koreans. Even though they were our fellow countrymen, the northerners were "red devils" with horns protruding from their foreheads. I found this description puzzling and even amusing at times, but prior to the outbreak of war, the political situation didn't matter to me one way or the other. These red-devil Koreans with horns lived far from my village.

The war forced many of the martial arts associations (known as "kwans") that had become popular following the ousting of the Japanese to close their doors because their instructors had been drafted into the military. Consequently, hundreds of martial arts students had to put their training on the back burner. However, the war proved helpful to the Korean martial arts. In 1952, President Syngman Rhee watched a half-hour demonstration and was so impressed by a student breaking 13 roofing tiles that he ordered all soldiers to receive training in the martial arts of our country.

If there was a positive outcome to becoming a soldier and joining the war, it was that I didn't want to be excluded. Master Ko had worked hard to raise my level of self-worth and my strong desire to be a *part of* rather than *apart from*. I knew I had come a long way toward getting well and being treated as a normal human being. So while I certainly didn't want to be separated from my family, I was looking forward to being able to say, "I am a soldier standing beside the others in uniform." I didn't have the slightest clue about the formidable enemy I was about to find myself up against.

The North Korean army was in every sense of the word a *professional* military. Of the more than 90,000 troops, a third of them had fought in the Chinese civil war, and the remaining two-thirds were whipped into fighting shape before they ever crossed the 38th parallel. This war machine was so well oiled and efficient that they completely destroyed five Republic of Korea (ROK) divisions in as many weeks.

Unlike the North Korean army, which was professionally trained by the Soviets and given an arsenal of sophisticated weaponry, South Korea's army entered the war with shortages of manpower, finances, food, and officers trained in the tactics of war. To illustrate how poorly skilled the bulk of the South Korean army was, new recruits were trained to be full-fledged soldiers in *three days.*

The morning after I was spirited away from my mother, my first day of training to be a soldier began. Essentially, it amounted to how to wear a uniform and how to bow and salute. That was all. My second day of training focused on how to load, aim, and shoot a gun. On my third day of training, I was taught to march, crawl, and run for my life in a zigzag pattern. And that was it—those three days were the full extent of my military training.

Now that I was a soldier, my superiors sent me to specialty school, where in one day I was trained to be a field medic. My job was simple: I was shown how to attend to soldiers wounded in combat—I was to treat everything from bayonet injures to bullets in skulls. And my medic's bag was as deficient as everything else in the South Korean army, amounting to two quarts of iodine and several fistfuls of sterile rags.

On the battlefield, wherever I encountered bleeding, I was to drench the wound with iodine, and then do whatever was necessary to stop the blood flow. My choices were to apply a tourniquet, which almost always meant a subsequent amputation (if not death), or to stuff the wound with rags. Wishing the wounded or dying man good luck, I would then move on to the next screaming soldier.

When I wasn't being a medic, I was trying to look and act like an infantryman. However, there was a major problem when it came to firepower. While all soldiers were equipped with bullets that were loaded eight to a clip, not everyone had a rifle. So when we found our unit under attack, the man with the gun would fire his bullets at the enemy, throw the rifle to the next guy, and immediately start preparing his next round of bullets for when the rifle returned (if it ever did). The second man would fire his bullets, then throw the rifle to the next man, and we'd continue down the line in this manner. I cannot begin to describe the utter sense of helplessness of sitting in a trench with several rounds of bullets, as the enemy was charging from all directions, and having to wait for a rifle to arrive in working order. It was not uncommon for a rifle to jam on one soldier, and it became his responsibility to dismantle the weapon and get it back into working order while his comrades listened to enemy bullets whizzing over their heads and ricocheting off their helmets.

This situation would be further complicated when a rifle would fly through the air and fall at a soldier's feet, and he would discover, much to his horror, that the weapon was one that had been confiscated from the enemy and was Soviet-made. The problem, of course, was that many bullets weren't generic—American-made bullets didn't necessarily fit Soviet-made rifles, and vice versa. So a soldier could have his pockets brimming with bullets, but if the wrong weapon arrived, he would be unable to defend himself. He'd be better off storming out of the trenches and taking his chances attacking the enemy with the bayonet. (On more than one occasion I held a gun on a captured enemy soldier that wasn't even loaded!)

We really did need help, and we prayed that the desperately needed U.S. troops would arrive soon. Even though our squad could go for days without encountering live fire, we faced two worse enemies every day: the bitter Korean winter and borderline starvation. After going several days without food, we would prepare what we called "tongue soup." The tongue was not that of an animal, but the tongue of our boots. This delicacy was prepared by first packing someone's helmet full of snow and then placing it over fire. When the water began to boil, we added several tongues that we had cut from our boots, along with whatever scrub vegetation we could scrounge up. We'd sit around and watch this horrid-smelling concoction brew for 15 minutes, and then divvy up the soup. We felt that the principal nourishment would come from the boot tongues because they were cowhide, so in a sense it was like beef. Other days my only meal would be several helmets full of snow.

Perhaps the most pathetic irony of all was that once a man or boy became a soldier in uniform, he was subject to becoming a soldier in either army. One day he could find himself fighting alongside the South Korean forces; if captured, the next day he became a soldier in the North Korean army. As a result, it was common for brothers and fathers to be fighting one another on opposite sides of any particular battle, and then a month later find themselves having again switched sides.

The blowing up of the Han River bridge in June 1950 was the first of a long string of war atrocities alleged to have been committed by both sides. The North Korean army routinely tortured and mutilated prisoners. Not uncommon was their practice of tying the hands of their captives behind their backs and then mowing them down with submachine gunfire. Many of their prisoners were brutally castrated without any anesthetic; still others who refused to talk under interrogation had their tongues cut out.

During the three years that I fought in the Korean War, I walked to the gates of hell and back. In fact, I sometimes think that I walked through hell and came out the other side. Yet I have often made the statement that my martial arts training saved my life. My reference is not to the physical moves that I was taught—after all, punches and flying kicks are no match for sniper bullets fired by an unseen enemy or high explosives that can blow a man to smithereens in an instant. What saved my life was the mind-set that Master Ko instilled in me at a young age. I was determined not to come home in a body bag.

I had triumphed over many physical and mental disabilities before fighting in the Korean War. The rocks that were thrown at me by the kids in my neighborhood were a far greater adversary than anything that was hurled at me by the North Korean army. From the first bullet fired at me, I knew that I was not going to become a statistic of that war. Deep in my soul, I knew I had a destiny to fulfill, even though I didn't know what it was as yet. When I was under heavy fire, and the adrenaline was soaring through my veins, I often saw the master's face and heard his voice repeat what he so often said in class: "Put your life on the line, son." That constant reminder ignited a will to survive that proved to be stronger than the determination of the North Korean army's to kill me.

By far the greatest opposition I faced in the Korean War was loneliness. I was only 15 years old when I entered the war, and prior to being drafted I had never been separated from my parents and siblings. When I struggled to find myself in early childhood, the loneliness that plagued me inevitably drove me to the banks of the Golden River, which was the only place in my world that offered me any peace. Now here I was fighting to survive the battlefields without the comfort and security of home. Letters written to my mother, father, and siblings went unanswered. I had no idea what had become of my family, and I feared that my older brother might have been killed in action. For three years, the loneliness that I fought was incredibly overwhelming at times. If and when this war ever ended, assuming I were to survive, where was I to go? I lived with the tremendous fear that I would be going home to an empty village. But I was determined to keep fighting in the hopes that one day my family would all be reunited.

The Korean War is said to have been the most atrocious and bloody war in the history of modern warfare. In addition to 1,600,000 soldiers who gave their lives, and another 420,000 missing in action, it is estimated that more than ten million Koreans were separated from their families during the three years of the war. Many were never reunited. Tragically, at the war's end, there was no clear-cut victor. North Korea returned to being ruled by the Communists, while South Korea remained a part of the free world.

It took two years before my family was fully reunited. Sorrowfully, my older sister, Sun, died during the war, and my brother Duk was wounded in battle. Yet he survived—along with my mother and father, the twins, and me. I don't believe that, as a country, Korea will ever be the same. The blood of hundreds of thousands of dead soldiers will forever remain a part of her soil.

chapter 5 :::
Bringing Balance to my Unbalanced Art

:::
:::

At the end of the Korean War in 1953, I returned to civilian life in Ansung. I was 18 years of age and eager to resume my martial arts training full time. Not surprisingly, my father had other ideas. Having been an educator for most of his adult life, he insisted that I enroll in college and study economics. So I reluctantly began to take classes at Korea University in Seoul.

I spent every minute of my free time, however, training with Master Ko. Because the martial arts had been taught in the military during the war, many Koreans were curious about this ancient and mystical form of self-defense. Therefore, the master asked me to open a studio in the town of Sin Kil Dong (right outside Seoul).

My father voiced his concern that opening a martial arts studio would detract from my studies, but I was insistent. Besides, he had known for years that the martial arts were my only true passion in life and that Master Ko's wish was my command. Eventually my father acquiesced, provided that I remain in school. I agreed to this and relocated to Sin Kil Dong, where I lived in the back of a small, dilapidated storefront.

I attended college classes in the mornings and worked afternoons and evenings fixing up the studio. Everything was in disrepair—besides installing new flooring and plaster to the walls, I patched up the leaky roof and painted both the interior and exterior of the building. It was hard work, but with every new nail pounded in and every stroke of the paintbrush, I could sense my master's presence and his approval. The process of giving birth to this new studio brought me great joy.

Throughout the renovation, townspeople would occasionally wander in and ask questions. While they seemed very interested in having a new martial arts studio in Sin Kil Dong, when I told them that I was going to be the instructor, they would look at me funny. At 18 years of age, I just didn't fit their preconceived image of a black belt martial arts instructor, even in light of the fact that I had survived three years of fighting in the Korean War. I guess they expected a mystical figure dressed in robes and sporting a long beard. (This was the same problem that the legendary Bruce Lee encountered when he began teaching kung fu in the United States in 1959. Because he was only 18 at the time, hardly anyone took him seriously. He soon proved them wrong.) Regardless, the suspicions of the people of Sin Kil Dong didn't concern me. I knew that when the time came, I would be able to prove myself.

A few blocks from the studio was a movie theater that featured an afternoon matinee and two showings in the evenings. I made a point to be standing outside the theater when the moviegoers walked out. I would greet them wearing my martial arts uniform and hand them flyers and my business card. In Korea, it is not customary for a martial artist to wear his uniform in public. I suppose I came off as some sort of street preacher, and many said I was crazy and had no shame. I didn't care. Martial arts was my passion and my life, and I was willing to do whatever was necessary to bring people to the studio to at least see what I had to offer.

The first day I opened for business, 15 students signed up for the introductory course. I estimated that each of these students had 15 other people waiting to hear the reviews of the new kid on the block. Everything was on the line; it was sink or swim. So I pulled out all the stops and gave these 15 novice students a crash course in martial arts that made their hair stand up on end. The next day I had another 20 students. By the end of the month, I turned out to be a bigger success than I could have ever imagined, and I soon realized that I needed help. I just couldn't teach all these classes and keep up with my college studies.

As time went by, my reputation as a formidable martial artist and gifted teacher began to circulate in and around Sin Kil Dong. Soon, other black belts sought me out and began studying under me. By the end of six months, I had an adequate teaching staff, was generating enough revenue to open a second studio for Master Ko, and found a nice house to live in. Over the next three years I opened six more studios throughout the surrounding areas of Sin Kil Dong. All seven studios ended up having a total enrollment of more than 5,000 students.

At that time, there were five major associations trying to gain leadership and control of the Korean martial arts. Of the five, Master Ko agreed to affiliate our chain of studios with the Korean Tang Soo Do Association, which was founded in 1953 by Hwang Kee. (As a footnote, in 1960 the Korean government registered Tang Soo Do as "the traditional Korean Martial Art.")

In the 1950s, when the general Korean population first became exposed to the martial arts, it was amazing what power they gave the few who held the rank of black belt. With the physical strength of ten men and the ability to kill another human being in mere seconds, many of these black belts were thought to be superhuman and were even worshiped like gods . . . and I was one of them.

By the time I reached the age of 20, such worship turned out to be a double-edged sword. With more than 5,000 students under my control, I was a powerful person in the Seoul martial arts community. Because so many people were treating me as if I were an ancient emperor, I began to act like a dictator. My martial arts had become unbalanced due to youth and pride. Consequently, my personality and presence were made up almost entirely of the hard (yang) side of the yin/yang symbol—I was short-tempered, demanding, and argumentative, like a fire-breathing dragon lashing its tail out at the world. In a strange way, my arrogance only served to make my students idolize me more. Everywhere I went, people bowed to me, and no one dared open his or her mouth without my permission.

I was walking along a dark path and heading for trouble.

One day I was working in my office when suddenly the entire building seemed to shake on its foundation. I knew immediately that this had been caused by the entire class falling to its knees. I knew of only one individual who could cause such a response just by his appearance. I opened my office door to see Master Ko standing in the entryway to the studio. Out on the training area, more than 100 students were hunched over their knees on the hardwood floor, bowing to the master.

Moments later Master Ko and I sat in the office and spoke privately. He was pleased by the progress of the studio and had an assignment for me. Our relationship had not changed since my boyhood years—even in light of all my accomplishments, the master still had absolute power.

"I have something I need you to do," he began.

"Yes, sir."

"There is a school not far from here with students who are ready to be tested. I want you to go there on my behalf."

"Yes, sir," I answered. I tried to get a better description of the school, but the master did not give it a name and implied only that it was somehow affiliated with him.

"I want you to leave early tomorrow morning," he continued. "The school is about 100 miles to the east. You can make most of the trip by bus and taxi, but the last 30 miles you will have to travel on foot."

On the surface this didn't seem too bad. Another one of the master's students, Yeon, was to accompany me and assist with the testing. Yeon was in excellent physical condition, so I knew that he would be able to keep up with me. Besides, I'd have someone to talk to.

The next morning, Yeon and I took off. The bus was crowded and noisy, and the taxi was driven by a man who chain-smoked and smacked a mouthful of fruity bubble gum—at the same time—throughout the entire two-hour drive. Yet Yeon and I passed the time by talking about the royal greeting that we were sure awaited our arrival. Following the testing, we envisioned a grand ceremony with everyone bowing to us and filling our plates with delicacies and our glasses with rice wine.

The taxi driver drove us to the end of the paved road, where the beginning of a four-foot-wide dirt path headed off at a right angle and led up a mountain. Something didn't seem right, so I double-checked the map that Master Ko had given me. The driver assured me that we were in the right place, even though the master's drawing made it appear that the dirt path was as wide as the paved road.

I paid the driver and watched him drive off. Yeon and I grabbed our duffel bags and jugs of water and headed up the trail. It was around 10 A.M., so I estimated that we would arrive at our final destination in about six hours. An hour later I began to wonder if we would ever arrive at all.

I had underestimated the punishing Korean summer heat. By 11 A.M. the temperature had exceeded the 100-degree mark and the humidity was so thick that a man sitting on his living-room sofa could have watched the wallpaper fall from the walls. Worst of all were the insects that buzzed around like kamikaze pilots, attacking anything that moved. As for ground troops, I had never seen so many lizards, snakes, and mangy field rodents in one place; and under my feet I could hear the crunch of bugs, some as large and hard as jawbreakers. And the smell of animal waste was horrible.

Yeon and I made little forward progress, since after another hour we began to run low on water. As a result, we spent nearly as much time searching for water as we did heading up that mountain. Two hours later we noticed buzzards circling overhead. It wasn't likely that they had us on their radar screens (not yet, anyway), but the sight of them caused Yeon and me to begin arguing, each blaming the other for everything that had gone wrong. We finally reached our destination around midnight— tired, hungry, thirsty, and covered with insect bites.

It was obvious that this little village had rolled up its streets hours earlier. There was no greeting party—not so much as a welcoming banner with our names on it. We found our way to the small residence of Mr. Kwan, whose name was given to me by Master Ko. I walked onto the darkened porch and pounded on the door.

Moments later the door opened to reveal a man dressed in a scruffy bathrobe, wiping sleep from his eyes. "Master Yu?" he asked groggily.

"Were you expecting someone else at this hour?"

"No, sir. Of course not. Please come in."

Yeon and I entered, dropped our bags on the floor, and immediately demanded water. For the next few minutes we drank several quarts between us, after which Kwan explained that his students had waited for us at the studio until 10 P.M., at which point they had gone home. They would return tomorrow for testing at whatever time was convenient for us.

"My associate and I are tired," I replied bluntly. "We will test at two o'clock tomorrow afternoon and then attend whatever awards ceremony you have planned."

Kwan bowed respectfully. "As you wish, Master Yu. Will you be staying overnight tomorrow?"

"That is correct." I didn't have to consult Yeon. There was no way that either of us was heading back down that ghostly path at night with our stomachs filled with rice wine.

"We are honored," Kwan said. He offered us a kettle of hot water to clean our hands and faces, and a late dinner that amounted to warmed-over rice with shrimp, pickled radish, kimchee, and a pot of ginseng tea. After our meal, we were shown to a small guest room, where Kwan had made up two surplus cots from the Korean War, each with a lumpy pillow and a moth-eaten blanket.

Yeon and I dozed off, convinced that the worst was behind us.

The next day Kwan took us to his "martial arts studio," which was not a formal school by anyone's standards, but a small, cleared area in the back of his family-owned grocery store. The dimly lit room was cluttered with sacks of rice, stacks of canned goods, and crates of wilting vegetables. Standing at attention in the middle of the room, dressed in uniform, were Kwan's students—all six of them!

I couldn't believe my eyes. "This is *it?* Only six students!" I exploded before anyone could respond. This was not a martial arts studio! This was a joke! Six students training in a ten-foot-square area in the back of Kwan's tiny market out in the middle of nowhere? I agreed to go ahead with the testing as Master Ko had requested, but I was going to get to the bottom of who had misled the master into believing that "Kwan's Korean Martial Arts Studio" was a respectable school.

"Line up! Attention!" I shouted to no one in particular.

To this day I can still see the frozen expressions on the faces of Kwan and his six students. Over the next two hours I became an uncaged tiger, striking the students with kicks and punches and bouncing them off the walls like rag dolls. Even Yeon was shocked and chose to stand off to one side for the entire testing period and never said a word. At the end of the testing, I passed four of the six students.

A half hour later Yeon and I left town, declining to take part in the awards ceremony scheduled for later that night. I wanted to get back to Sin Kil Dong, and I didn't care what horrors I might encounter along the way. I felt as if the blood of ten angry mountain lions was racing in my veins. I needed to get back to where I would be treated with the respect and admiration befitting a black belt of my caliber.

The evening was cool and moonlit, so Yeon and I found our return trip to be much easier than the uphill journey we had made the day before. Upon arriving in Sin Kil Dong late that evening, I was relieved to be back home, and I slept like a king.

Late the following morning, Master Ko and I met. He seemed more content on listening than talking, sensing that I needed to vent.

"Six students, can you imagine? In back of Kwan's market," I spat. "The place looked more like an abandoned bomb shelter than a martial arts studio. All that way—30 miles, walking up some mountain under a scorching sun just to test six students. I hope that when you talked with this Kwan fellow this morning he apologized for misleading everyone."

Master Ko's thoughts seemed to be elsewhere. "Yes. Well, Mr. Kwan was quite upset. He felt that he had dishonored you and Yeon. I guess you lost your temper and took it out on his market—and his students," he said without expression.

"That's correct. I demonstrated on a 50-pound sack of rice that was held by two of the students. I hit that sack with a spinning kick, and it exploded. I also kicked out a wooden post that held up a section of the roof that fell on Kwan and his guys. I was plenty mad, all right."

I elected to drop the matter of how Kwan managed to convince Master Ko to send two of his black belts 100 miles to test six students.

I was satisfied that the master was pleased that I had disciplined these students and their teacher, so it came as no surprise when he appeared a week later with a new assignment.

"I need you to travel to a distant village and open a school," he said, handing me another map.

I could hardly believe that I would be traveling up that same path again, only this time breaking off at the halfway point—and I would be alone.

The master pointed to a particular spot on the map and said, "This village is about ten miles to the north of where these two roads meet. I understand that the people there are in need of learning the art."

I could tell that Master Ko was excited, and I promised him that I would carry out his wish. I left the next morning with the same duffel bag and water jug, and a small amount of money for opening the school. The master thought I would be gone for about a month, and he told me that he would stay in touch with his "sources" in that area and join me when my mission was completed.

Following another tough journey, I finally reached my destination, tired but eager to get busy establishing a school. Like the humiliating circumstances that I encountered at Kwan's market, I soon became aware of some problems. To begin with, the population of this entire village amounted to about 200 people. This was hardly a large enough base from which to recruit students for a standard martial arts school. Far worse was the fact that this village resembled a monastery. It was a communal farming village where everyone paid a lot of attention to the singing birds and blossoming flowers. Everyone seemed to walk in slow motion, as if in meditation. These people were totally opposed to violence—to raise one's voice was a sin, even in private to another family member. I fully expected the Dalai Lama to appear at any moment.

Conditions quickly went from bad to worse. I had to find a place to teach, but none existed. The entire village belonged to everyone, and the idea of leasing commercial space was completely foreign, if not disturbing, to these people.

Over the next few days, I tried to explain to these farmers the benefits of learning the martial arts. But the more persistent I became, the more disinterested they were. After a while, they would look at the ground or gaze up at the mountain when I began one of my lectures. Sometimes they would just turn and walk away, leaving me in mid-sentence.

Unlike the royal life I had been living in Sin Kil Dong, I was anything but a king in this place. No one was offering to bring me my meals with their heads bowed. What little food I had brought with me was almost gone. And the money I had was worthless because there were no markets in this village—only one big communal farm.

One morning I finally blew my stack. I grabbed one of the younger men and began yelling, "Don't you know who I am? I am a black belt in the martial arts! I came all this way to teach you guys! If you were back in Sin Kil Dong, you'd all be on a two-year waiting list! And by the way, I fought for three years in the war so that you people could continue to live a peaceful life up on this mountain tilling the soil and thinking about your inner souls or whatever it is you do here! Are you paying attention?"

This only served to get me in more trouble. An older woman immediately came at me with a broom, and in the days that followed, the villagers began throwing salt at me, which was their way of warding off evil spirits. I had reached a dead end, yet I had no choice but to wait for Master Ko to arrive.

Another six weeks passed, and I became desperate when winter began to set in. I sectioned off a wooded space outside the village, where I constructed a primitive lean-to and survived off the natural vegetation and the occasional fish I caught in a nearby stream. Finally, the harsh winter proved to be too much for me. I spent all of my waking hours shivering, and I began to lose weight because the vegetation, buried deeper and deeper in the falling snow, became very scarce.

Although the villagers were displeased that I had remained in their midst, they were humane. Soon they began to leave small amounts of food, dry wood, and clothing outside my crude dwelling. Occasionally I would leave my lean-to and wander into their village, where I strolled around their streets with an unfriendly look on my face. They continued to ignore me, which led me to conclude that their kindness had been inspired by the fear of having to bury this evil intruder inside the boundaries of their peaceful village.

In Sin Kil Dong, I had been a king, and now I was nothing. I was worse off than a slave, because these people wouldn't even use me to work. Many times I thought of leaving, but I knew that Master Ko would only send me back. The reality that my beloved martial art was worthless to these people made me feel that I had returned to my childhood role of the Ugly Boy who had nothing to offer.

When I didn't hear from Master Ko for months, I sank into a deep depression and became willing to die alone in my lean-to. Then one night as I lay in the darkness, I thought, *Okay, this is the day the end has come to me. I'm going to die alone in this dark lean-to beside this icy river. Nobody will find me for days, and when they do, no one will care.* But just as I felt as though I were falling off to sleep for the last time, I heard the master's voice cry, "You put your life on the line! What are you afraid of? Why are you giving up?"

The words were so clear that I thought Master Ko was standing over me, but when I opened my eyes, no one was there. Moments later the truth of those words hit me: I had *not* put my life on the line. Instead, I had come to this village expecting the people to pay homage to me based on my past accomplishments. I expected them to show me respect and bow to me because of my superior knowledge of the martial arts. Yet the truth was, I had not earned any of this. The next morning I returned to the village, having made a promise to myself that I wouldn't leave these people until I had given them something of value.

There is an old saying that says, "When the student is ready, the teacher will appear." Perhaps in this case, the opposite was true—when the teacher is ready, the student will appear.

Not long after my arrival six months before, an adolescent boy had begun following me around at a safe distance. I never noticed him before, but now he stood out among the villagers. He had been born with one leg rotated outward, which caused him to walk unevenly and one side of his body to become overdeveloped.

Deep inside he must have known that I could help him. Seeing a major change in my personality, the boy approached me and asked if I would teach him, being careful to avoid any reference to learning how to fight. He was asking for me to teach him to have better control of his body movement. Later that day, I talked with the boy's parents, and they agreed to allow their son to train with me, but within strict guidelines.

I readily identified with the emotional problems this boy had endured for the better part of his young life, and over the next six weeks we became practically inseparable. Focusing on the underdeveloped side of his body, I worked with him on stretching the ligaments and tendons and strengthening the muscles of his twisted leg. I taught him how to balance all his weight over on one leg and to jump, which he had never done before. After a month he was jogging with me in the mornings. Soon his personality changed from that of a withdrawn, unhappy child to one who greeted each day with enthusiasm and gratitude. Thankfully, his changed personality didn't go unnoticed by the villagers. Eventually other parents brought their children, and not long thereafter, the elderly began to arrive, wanting to train. No longer did I have any interest in teaching these students how to kick and punch and break boards, for now I saw that this was not what they wanted—or needed.

I eventually left my lean-to and moved into a small room in the home of one of the village families. Life was good. Never before had I experienced such peace of mind. I forgot about my extravagant, egotistical existence back in Sin Kil Dong; I didn't miss its modern conveniences or its fast pace. These people never called me "Master"—instead, they referred to me only as "Teacher Yu."

At some point I stopped counting days and began viewing the passage of time in terms of seasons. I awoke one spring morning to learn that Master Ko had arrived in the village. When he saw what I had accomplished and learned that I had more than 60 students, he said, "I am pleased by what I see and what these people have told me about you. You are a different person, son. Before, your being was out of balance—far too much yang, and not enough yin. Eventually this would have destroyed you. Now you have become a complete martial artist. I hope that you appreciate the lessons you have learned. Anyway, your work here is finished. In the morning you will return with me to Yong Dung Po."

The master's mention of our departure came without warning and left me speechless. I truly did not want to leave this new life to which I had become accustomed. At least not this quickly.

That afternoon I taught the villagers for the last time. I told them that I would be going away in the morning and that although Master Ko had no plans of sending another instructor to their village, I was convinced in my heart that a teacher would appear to carry on with the work I had started. I closed the class for the last time with the usual salutation of respect, and then we hugged one another and shared our tears together.

In 1956, I returned to the life I had left almost a year earlier in Sin Kil Dong. It was very difficult. No longer was I attracted to the constant praise and worship shown to me by my students. The strong yang side of my martial art had now been balanced with the softer yin. I had attained a higher level—yet I still had further to go and more lessons to learn.

Over the next few years, martial arts tournaments became popular throughout Korea and neighboring Japan. I maintained a busy schedule, dividing my time between my rigorous training, running my chain of studios, competing in tournaments, and finishing college. Of my many tournament victories, the most prestigious included being crowned Grand Champion in the Korean-Japanese Invitational and the Okinawan National Championships. Although it was a time of great celebration and joy, there was sadness looming on the horizon.

In the spring of 1962, Master Ko summoned me to my birthplace of Kyung Ki-Do. I immediately traveled to his home, and we sat together on the front porch. Even though he was now age 70 and his health was failing, he spoke clearly. "Son, do you remember the day that we journeyed to the ocean, when you were a young boy?" he asked.

"Yes, sir. You taught me about all the fish in the ocean," I fondly recalled.

"Yes. And you wanted to become as big and strong as the whale, so that one day you could swim across the water to America. Do you remember?"

"I remember."

After a long, thoughtful pause, he looked straight into my eyes and said, "I think now is the time, son. I want you to go to America and spread our art. I want you to do this with my blessing and in my name."

I was instantly filled with conflicting emotions. I was so incredibly honored, and at the same time totally confused. I was neither Master Ko's most senior student nor his best. I came to him as a retarded kid, the clumsy one who only wanted to be a part of the group. Still, he chose me to carry his dream to America. The thought filled me with fear—what a tremendous burden of responsibility to bear. Yet whatever the master's reasons, I loved him and knew that I would have to try with all my strength and determination.

This was the last conversation I had with Master Ko, who passed away four days later.

In my mind, these words kept repeating themselves over and over: *The master's wish is my command.* Perhaps he had handed me the torch because he knew that above all else I was not a quitter or a loser, and that I would put my life on the line, for him and his art.

chapter 6 :::
Coming
to
America

:::

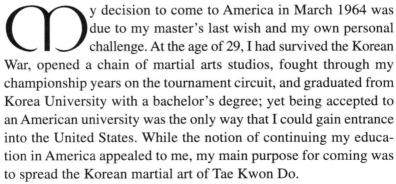

y decision to come to America in March 1964 was
due to my master's last wish and my own personal
challenge. At the age of 29, I had survived the Korean
War, opened a chain of martial arts studios, fought through my
championship years on the tournament circuit, and graduated from
Korea University with a bachelor's degree; yet being accepted to
an American university was the only way that I could gain entrance
into the United States. While the notion of continuing my education in America appealed to me, my main purpose for coming was
to spread the Korean martial art of Tae Kwon Do.

I felt prepared to come to America—my only fear was that I
didn't speak English. I was able to verbalize only a few dozen
words and could read a little, so I would have to rely almost entirely
on my tiny pocket dictionary. Add to that a few other gestures

common to international language, and that was the extent of my ability to communicate in America.

In the mid-1960s, Korea was still a very poor country, and residents who left were not allowed to take more than $50 with them. Although I had little money, I didn't look poor. My parents and other relatives chipped in to provide me with a fairly nice wardrobe that included a few suits, a half-dozen shirts, a sweater, and two pairs of new shoes. The day before I left, my mother paid for a haircut, and my father gave me an inexpensive but attractive wristwatch and ring.

The morning of my flight, I arrived at the airport in Seoul two hours early and was checked through customs. My passport was in order, as was the visa that had been issued to me by the United States. The only problem was that I was not allowed to work in America. I had to be supported by some sort of sponsorship, although I was assured by other students that no one in the U.S. would check. Months earlier I had sent my school transcripts and paperwork to the University of California at Berkeley, so they were expecting me in September. This meant that I had six months to get accustomed to the United States—all I had to do was survive until then.

After bidding my family good-bye, I boarded a Northwest Airlines four-engine plane that looked to be close to retirement, and anxiously strapped myself into my seat near the back of the plane. The only airplanes I had seen at this point were downed helicopters and fighter planes during the Korean War. So most of the experiences I had included the twisted remains of burning aircraft and the smell of jet fuel.

The plane took off normally, but because it was my first time, I could feel my throat drop into the pit of my stomach from nerves. Minutes later, we leveled off at 30,000 feet, and I began to breathe a little easier.

The flight had stopovers in Japan and Hawaii before reaching its final destination in San Francisco. I spent most of the flight staring out the window—practically all that I saw for the entire 11-hour flight was the sky and ocean, so I had plenty of time to think. By nightfall I would be arriving in San Francisco with a fairly simple agenda. I had only to find a place to sleep and eat for a few days, after which I would have ample time to register for school and find part-time work for six months before classes began in September. Compared to the life I had left behind in Korea, I fully expected that the next six months in America were going to be a vacation.

Over the years I had heard many good things about this "Golden Land of Opportunity," especially from the American soldiers who were stationed in Korea. According to them, there would be plenty of work waiting for me, and most Americans would go out of their way to greet me with a friendly smile and a warm handshake. I was looking forward to seeing the Golden Gate Bridge, riding the trolley to the top of Nob Hill, and eating fresh crab at Fisherman's Wharf. I was so excited that in the month prior to leaving Seoul, I had learned to hum "God Bless America."

It was early evening when we finally landed at San Francisco International Airport. The terminal was really crowded, but I managed to make my way through customs without any problem. An hour later, I stood at the front of the airport, holding my two bags. Everyone was racing around the place as if they knew where they were going, but I didn't have a clue as to my next destination. No one had made arrangements for anyone to meet me because my family had neither friends nor relatives in San Francisco. Although I saw a good number of Asians inside the terminal, I didn't see one Korean. I later learned that the Korean consulate had fewer than 100 Koreans registered in the entire Bay Area.

Over the next hour, I ventured outside the terminal building several times, only to become more overwhelmed. People, cars, and buses were racing in all directions, and uniformed police were set on keeping everyone moving. My biggest concern was that there were no signs indicating lodging or stores outside the terminal—just more airport. With no idea where to go, I hustled back into the building.

After wandering around for another half hour, I found my way to a row of counters where large advertisements appeared to have something to do with lodging. I took a nearby seat and started leafing through my pocket dictionary. It turned out that I was right. According to my dictionary, there were three types of lodging in America—hotels, motels, and inns. Hotels were the most expensive, motels were for middle-class travelers, and poor people stayed at inns. I thought, *Hey, I'm halfway there—I know that I belong at an inn. Now all I need to figure out is which one.*

Eventually I narrowed my choices down to the Holiday Inn. Why? Because I was a poor guy with no job, which meant I was on *vacation,* which was another English word for *holiday.* Relieved that I was making progress, I grabbed my bags and approached the agent who was working at the counter. It was there that I received my first friendly smile and helping hand.

Moments later I stood at the curb outside the terminal, where a minibus from the Holiday Inn pulled up alongside me. The driver popped open the side door, jumped out from behind the wheel, loaded my bags, and welcomed me aboard. As we pulled away from the airport, I thought, *Wow, America is good to me! This is my kind of poor! They're picking me up for free, carrying my bags, and now I'm relaxing in a heated bus and enjoying the passing scenery while soft music plays through a tiny speaker directly over my head.*

Before I knew it, the driver pulled up in front of the Holiday Inn, which was located in a nice part of the city. The people who worked there appeared thrilled by my arrival. Everyone smiled as they toted my bags and opened doors for me. The beaming man at the front desk greeted me like a long-lost friend as he slid a registration form in front of me and handed me an attractive pen. This was some kind of treatment for someone with no job, and now I knew why people wanted to come to America. As I was filling out the registration card, the desk clerk said, "Would you prefer to sleep on a king?"

I had absolutely no idea what he was asking me. I hauled out my dictionary and asked him to repeat the question several times, which he did. It still didn't make any sense to me. Confused, I concluded that he was asking if I wanted to sleep *with* a king! I said, "No king!"

The man offered a courteous smile and replied, "Fine. Would you prefer a queen?"

Now I was totally lost. Can you imagine—a poor guy just arrives from Korea and is being offered a bed with an American queen?

"No, no—no queen!" I said, my face reddening.

"Then you want a double."

That didn't sound as bad. My dictionary defined *double* as "two of something," so I thought that maybe there were two beds, one stacked on top of the other. Anyway, I agreed to the double.

I rode with the bellboy up a shiny brass elevator, and then we walked down a hall with plush carpet and beautiful art hanging on the walls. We finally reached my room, where the bellboy placed my bags inside and then stood in front of me with his hand held out. Without a thought, I shook the man's hand and thanked him in my broken English. Later, when I learned about the American custom of tipping, I was both ashamed and astounded, for here was just another example of how perfect America was. In Korea, people were lucky to have menial jobs; in America, not only did a person get paid by his employer, but he got all that extra money from the customers as well.

After the bellhop left, I saw the two double beds. The sight was unbelievable. I imagined getting up in the middle of the night for a glass of water, and when I came back, I could crawl into a fresh bed! I thought, *These Americans are fantastic. I have two beds!* At first, I thought the hotel clerk would be sending another guest to sleep in the other bed, so I waited a while for someone to arrive. When no one did, I finally turned in.

In Korea, one room routinely housed multiple families, including parents and children, and everyone slept in that one room. In addition, everyone had to share the same toilet, which was outside in the dirt. Koreans were that poor. Now here I was, one guy with *two* beds, his own private toilet, and a tub and sink with hot water that was clean enough to drink.

We had hotels in Korea, but they weren't anything like the lavish skyscrapers in America. They were more like boardinghouses. Some lucky person would get a bed, but almost everyone slept on the floor. In America, so I soon discovered, the situation was reversed: Practically everyone slept in a bed, and it was rare that anyone slept on the floor. And the bed was big enough to hold four or five people!

That night I didn't sleep well because the bed was so soft. And I awoke the next morning extremely hungry. There was a colorful menu on the table, but besides the pictures, I couldn't make sense of it. I walked out into the hallway and located a cleaning lady who was making the beds in one of the rooms. Through my usual flurry of hand gestures and a few words from my dictionary, I was able to convey to the woman that I was hungry.

There were three basic breakfasts featured on the menu—Breakfast Number 1, Breakfast Number 2, and Breakfast Number 3. I tried to figure out the differences, and in so doing, pointed at all three of them. The maid nodded politely like everyone else in that hotel, patted me on the back, and gave me the impression that she would take care of it.

A short while later, there was a gentle knock on the door, followed by the appearance of a man wearing a white coat. He wheeled in a long table that held enough food to feed half the South Korean army—pancakes, six eggs, French toast, bacon, sausage, three glasses of orange juice, fresh fruit, and two pots of coffee—all set on a white linen tablecloth and surrounded by shiny silverware, china, and a single yellow rose. This breakfast was fit for a king! With my mouth hung open, I scribbled my name on the check, shook the man's hand, and bid him farewell. Then I ate as much as I could and placed the rest in a plastic bag to eat later.

I was eager to get moving. If this was what America was all about, then I was ready to meet the people. In view of the way I had already been treated, it was clear that Americans thought I was an important person. Maybe by the end of the day I would meet the President!

I took a shower and splashed on some Aqua Velva aftershave and Vitalis hair tonic from the hotel's complimentary basket of toiletries. Knowing that I could come back and stay another night if I wanted, I packed my bags and headed for the main lobby. I felt like a millionaire.

The morning desk clerk greeted me with a smile and graciously handed me my bill. I took one glance at the total and couldn't believe my eyes. The total came to $53! I was more than shocked—I was horrified. Fifty-three U.S. dollars amounted to a small fortune in Korea. For $53 I could have spent an entire week in Seoul's finest boardinghouse. Besides what I felt was an extravagant room charge, I soon learned that I had mistakenly ordered three full breakfasts. But none of that mattered now. All I had was $50, which I grudgingly handed over, but the clerk wanted the other $3.

In trying to come up with a solution, I figured that my necktie was worth the difference. I removed it from my bag, placed it on the counter, and tried to explain to the clerk that the tie was worth at least three dollars. In Korea bartering worked, but not in America. The man looked at me and in so many words said no. I took that to mean that he was asking for more, so I removed a pair of brand-new shoes from my suitcase, placed them on the counter and, with the help of my dictionary, said, "What about shoes?"

The man showed even less interest in my footwear. He wanted three dollars cash. I tried to explain through body language and broken English that I simply did not have it. All I had was $50. We argued for at least 15 minutes, with my emptying most of the contents of my two bags on the counter. I was extremely disappointed. I mean, the night before they had asked me to sleep with a king or queen, and now they wouldn't accept my necktie and shoes for three dollars. That was what was running through my head—I was that naive.

The clerk finally said, "Lousy foreigners . . . get lost," and I was rudely shown the front door. To this day, I still remember those words and the way that clerk looked at me.

After being kicked out of the Holiday Inn, I recovered quickly. After all, I was still walking in the Golden Land of Opportunity, even if the clerk at the hotel had turned out to be a jerk. With both my bags in tow, I walked along the city sidewalks, fully expecting to be offered several jobs within the hour. I wasn't exactly sure how this was going to happen. Maybe people would just spot me from inside their stores and come racing outside to hire me. Or maybe cars would pull to the curb, and the drivers would offer me a job. I was just going by what those American soldiers had told me, what I had read about the easy life in America, and the many optimistic descriptions I had heard of this country over the years.

By 4 P.M. I was still unemployed and practically dead on my feet. I decided to enter several stores to ask for work, but the store owners only became frustrated by my inability to communicate and had no interest in hiring me. As darkness fell on the city, I was officially homeless and broke. I had been in America for about 24 hours, and had seen quite a reversal of fortune in that short period of time.

At the end of the first week, I had sold most of my clothing and extra pairs of shoes for hot dogs and hamburgers. At night I slept in Golden Gate Park. Since it was March, the temperature often dropped to near freezing. The cold was worse than I had experienced in Korea because of the wind-chill factor that was caused by the gusts blowing across the bay. It wasn't long before park rangers kicked me out of the park, and I found myself gravitating toward the seedier parts of the city. My next string of crash pads amounted to several 24-hour Laundromats, yet I was soon kicked out of those as well.

With no place to keep warm, I was forced to walk the streets at night. Like many large cities in the United States, there are parts of San Francisco that are continually alive with people, even in the predawn hours. I discovered that if I kept moving and gave the appearance that I was going somewhere and wasn't loitering, the police would leave me alone.

I soon realized that what little English I knew was practically useless. In Korea, we were taught the Japanese version of England's English, which, because of its bastardized intonations, sounded like another foreign language altogether in America. So I became desperate to learn American English. I was able to obtain a standard dictionary and went through it from A to Z, picking out one key word from each letter. From these 26 words, I then studied the dictionary again to find the opposite meaning of each of these words. For example, one of my words was "hello," which I paired with "good-bye." And so, I now had a total of 54 words, which I wrote on large index cards. I carried these cards with me everywhere and went though them several hundred times a day.

Besides these 54 words, I tried my hand at a few slang phrases that I picked up on the street. Around that time, *Rowan and Martin's Laugh-In* was very popular on television, and I immediately latched on to one of the show's catchphrases: "Sock it to me, baby." I studied my dictionary and couldn't figure out what that meant, but I used it anyway. (I'm sure you can imagine what embarrassing situations that phrase caused me.)

There were days when the sight and smell of a hot dog cooking on one of the city's corner stands drove me to seriously contemplate stealing. I just wanted to grab it and put it in my mouth, and I didn't care if the police arrested me. At least they would feed me in jail, and I would have a dry bed and heat at night. But I couldn't bring myself to steal. I hadn't come all this way to become an inmate of the city jail. And, of course, had I been arrested for anything, I would have been deported back to Korea.

I had to find a way to continue with my martial arts training, if for no other reason than to maintain my physical health. I would have a serious problem if I were to become sick with pneumonia or influenza, both of which were common among the homeless.

While Chinatown had its kung-fu schools, and Japantown had its karate dojos, I noticed that there weren't any Korean martial arts schools in San Francisco. I later discovered that in 1964 there were no Korean martial arts schools in California at all. And so, in lieu of training at a formal school, I trained by myself in Golden Gate Park. I regularly practiced forms; and performed many sets of kicks, punches, and blocks, using the trees as targets. In addition, I ran through a daily routine of calisthenics, jogged in the park, and often scaled up and down bleachers in a nearby stadium.

When I trained, people didn't know what I was doing—many thought I was a clown or something. Now and then some of the younger kids tried to mimic my movements. Occasionally people showed an interest in what I was doing, but for the most part I shunned them and kept to myself. I was still too proud to let anyone find out that I was homeless and hungry.

Hanging around Golden Gate Park was extremely hard for me. San Francisco has always had a large college community, and many students came to the park, especially when the weather was nice. I often observed lovers holding hands, young women pushing baby carriages, families enjoying picnics, and even people playing Frisbee with their dogs—all of them were living out the American dream, while I stood off in the shadows, fighting not to cry my eyes out. I had come to America with such good intentions and ended up as nothing more than a bum who spent his nights walking the streets and his days sleeping in the park, all the while panhandling for spare change or food.

I knew that if my situation became intolerable, I could go to the Korean consulate and admit that I didn't have the skills or courage to survive in America and tell them that I wanted to go home. The consulate would then call my parents and request that they arrange for my return flight home. Even though I had reached the point of regretting coming to America and truly wanted to return to Korea, I couldn't bring myself to go to the consulate. Before leaving Korea, I had become a famous martial arts champion and a college graduate. My father and mother had worked hard for years to bring back to our family name the dignity that the Japanese had taken away. Besides, I had told everyone that I wouldn't return before I had become a success in America, and I was too ashamed to admit that I had failed. I was going to stick this out, even if it meant dying on American soil.

I had to find a way to keep going. I reasoned that if I could make it to September when my college classes started, I would be okay. Even if I still didn't have lodging, I could sleep in the library and eat the food left on the tables of the school cafeteria. And by then maybe I would have made a friend or two. Making friends had never been easy for me, but now more than ever I was willing to do whatever it might take to do so.

I remember the day I hit rock bottom. When you're down and out and you still have a little something, *anything*—an extra shirt or pair of pants, a stash of food somewhere, even the affection of a homeless cat that meows at you when you're walking down an alley—there is still hope. You protect what little you have and are constantly on the watch for someone who might try to steal your goods. But when you reach the point that you have absolutely nothing but the clothes on your back and a single ID in your pocket—when that reality hits you, something happens and you flat-out stop caring.

I reached such a point one depressing May afternoon. My last pair of shoes had holes in them, my clothes were filthy, I was broke, and for two days I had tried to satisfy my hunger craving by gulping water from a gas-station hose. My life wasn't worth anything. The reality that I didn't know anybody and that no one cared whether I lived or died slammed into the depths of my soul. I would pass people in the street, and I would look at them and read their thoughts: *Who is that guy, that foreigner who sleeps in the park and always panhandles for food?* So when the day finally came that I reached an emotional and spiritual bottom, I stood at the entrance to a filthy alley located in one of the worst areas of the city and contemplated searching through my first garbage can to find nourishment.

chapter 7

Earning My Way and Restoring My Dignity

•••
•••

I survived on what little food I found in garbage cans for six weeks—which is how long it took me to figure out that there wasn't much sustenance to be found in most commercial and residential street garbage. Then one day, I noticed that there were hundreds of "human rats" roaming around San Francisco who disappeared at about the same time every night. They had to be going somewhere. So that night I decided to follow them, and I ended up in the alley behind a posh restaurant that was located on Montgomery Street.

An hour before the restaurant closed at 9 P.M., one of the waitresses came out the back door. She carried several sacks of trash that she threw into a row of garbage cans in the alley and then walked back into the restaurant for more. After she had made several trips, I noticed that the garbage cans were now loaded with leftover steaks, lobsters, baked potatoes, desserts, and even half-drunk bottles of wine.

This restaurant was known for serving large portions, so the unfinished dinners were gobbled up by the human rats waiting in the alley after closing. After seeing what was going on, I joined the pack, for there was plenty of food and drink for everybody. With the others, I dug through the cans for dinner, and after I had eaten, I filled up a plastic bag with food for the next day's breakfast and lunch.

I did this for two weeks. Then one night I arrived in the alley a couple of hours early. I just happened to be in this part of the city and found myself behind the restaurant on Montgomery Street around 6 P.M.

Since it was summer and still light outside, I could see the parking area beside the restaurant's main entrance from my perch in the alley. A steady stream of expensive cars was pulling in, and many nicely dressed people were entering the restaurant. Here again I was seeing the American dream unfolding before my eyes, but I wasn't a part of it. At first I was angry and even a little jealous, but then I started to feel bad because I realized that these people were actually paying for my food. It didn't matter what their jobs were—they could have been doctors and lawyers with big bank accounts or low-income people who had saved for a month to eat at this expensive restaurant.

I suddenly recalled the day when I had asked Master Ko if I could train with him. Twenty-three years later, his words still rang clearly in my ears: "None of my students train for free!" Tears began rolling down my cheeks as I realized how ashamed the master would have been to see me sitting in back of this restaurant, behaving like a human rat and waiting for a handout.

I looked around the alley. The place was a filthy mess: old mattresses, tires, broken furniture, wooden crates, beer cans and whiskey bottles, and even a dead cat were piled up in it. Years ago I paid for my lessons with Master Ko by cleaning up the school—maybe I could do the same thing here.

For the next two hours, I cleaned up that alley in back of the restaurant. I gathered up the junk that was scattered all over the place and put it all in one orderly pile. Next I picked up and placed all the loose paper and broken glass into one garbage can. I then neatly arranged all the cans and replaced the lids. After finishing the major cleanup, I swept the entire alley with a push broom that I found leaning against a back wall of a neighboring business.

None of the human rats who arrived that night appeared to notice the change in the alley, but the waitress who carried the garbage out of the restaurant did. She stopped and glanced up and down the alley before her eyes settled on the row of garbage cans that I had personally tidied up.

I slowly walked up to her, trying not to startle her. I smiled when she looked over at me. My English had improved somewhat: "See—look around. I clean up whole alley. Much better. You agree?"

The waitress wasn't frightened by me. "You're a little different from these other guys," she said. "You've got some character, that's for sure. What's your name?"

"Johnny," I replied, knowing that she would have a hard time pronouncing "Byong."

"Nice to meet you. I'm Vicky. You know, we won't pay you for doing all this work. I'm sorry, but—"

"I don't want to be paid," I interrupted.

"Oh? Then why did you do all this?"

The other human rats had moved closer, curious about our conversation. I chose to include them in my offer. "Please, no garbage in can. Too dirty in can."

"What do you want me to do?"

"Just put it here," I replied, as I held out my cupped hands. "That is all I am asking. That way we don't dig our food out of dirty cans."

"Fair enough." She smiled and handed me the first two bags.

"Tomorrow I come and clean everything up. Same deal, okay?" I asked, and she nodded.

We kept that deal for about a week. Vicky and I always greeted each other with a cheerful smile and friendly hello. Gradually the other workers in the restaurant began to treat me with a little respect and kindness because they could see that I was not comfortable with being fed for free.

One night, Vicky asked me to come into the restaurant. I was nervous, but I followed her through the back entrance. She led me to the kitchen, where the manager was standing. Behind him I could see stacks upon stacks of dirty dishes piled on both sides of the large sink. It also appeared that practically every pot and pan in the restaurant was dirty.

It turned out that the regular dishwasher had taken ill an hour before and had gone home. In his absence, other employees had tried to pitch in and help with the dishes, but the load proved to be too much. The place was still seating customers, and the chef was in such a rotten mood that he had started taking it out on the staff. Vicky had told the manager that I had been doing a great job cleaning up the alley, so he offered me a job washing dishes and scrubbing pots and pans. It was to be temporary, only until his regular dishwasher returned. He offered me minimum wage, which he would pay in cash.

I was so happy. Somebody finally needed my services and was asking me to work. After all these months, I had a purpose at last. I agreed to clean the kitchen.

"Great. But hurry it up," the manager said in a demanding voice. "You'll get paid when we close, after the kitchen is all clean for tomorrow."

He looked confused when I told him I didn't want money. Instead, all I wanted was to eat dinner in his restaurant. I'd be happy to do so after closing, and I had no problem eating in the kitchen. All I asked was that I sit at a table like most people in America, with a tablecloth and a proper place setting and napkin. I no longer felt like a nobody. I had value, and because of this I wanted to be treated accordingly. I wanted to earn the food I put in my mouth. When the manager agreed to do this for me, I was willing to work all night cleaning up his kitchen. We struck a deal that breathed life back into my body. American people finally needed me!

Like the fish back at the Golden River in my village, it was important for me to have a place to go, to know that somebody was waiting for me and that I was needed, and to have a place to relax and a place to work hard. I needed these things to feel human.

I went to work right away. I worked fast, yet I made sure that when the plates were dry, I could see my reflection in them. I was getting some degree of pride back, and I cleaned those dishes and pots and pans with a tremendous passion. This wasn't a job—it was an honor.

Two hours after closing, the kitchen was cleaned and ready for the next day. Off to one side was a beautifully set table with a nice dinner. Vicky had even placed a lit candle on the table.

I went to the restroom and washed my face and hands and fixed up my clothes as best I could. When I returned, I sat at that table and enjoyed one of the best meals of my life. I don't even recall what I ate—what was important was that it didn't come from garbage cans. I had earned this meal. For the first time in nearly four months, I was able to sit and eat like everybody else. I didn't have to crouch on the sidewalk or in the alley.

The restaurant's regular dishwasher never did return, so the manager asked me if I would like a permanent job washing dishes. I was so over-joyed that, after accepting, I excused myself to go to the restroom, where I broke down and cried. I hadn't begged them for the work; they had asked me. It was now official: I was no longer a human rat hang-ing around in the back alley. I was now a member of the team that worked inside the restaurant.

The manager asked me to come in at 10 A.M., but I was there at 9 to clean up the alley before starting my dishwashing duties. Meanwhile, I was still sleeping in the park and sometimes even in the alley itself, but no one at the restaurant knew.

I worked for minimum wage, which at that time was $1.20 an hour. After taxes, that meant I brought home $.98 an hour. Yet I worked 14 hours a day, always arrived on time, and never complained. Besides being a physically demanding job, back then there were no electric dishwashers. Everything was done by hand with a strong chemical and sponges. There were no gloves, just bare hands. I would put my hands in the chemical for ten hours every day, and my fingers would swell up to twice their normal size. And they hurt. But I always appreciated my job, and on payday I always thanked the owner for giving me the opportunity to work for him. Eventually, I graduated to the position of busboy.

In September of 1964, I began classes at UC Berkeley. When I attended college in Korea, I was a straight-A student. My school records had been so good that the University of California had accepted me as a student on a scholarship. What no one had anticipated, however, was the difficult language barrier I would face. I sort of understood the writing, and I could read a little with the help of my dictionary—but to express how I felt about any subject was impossible. The pressure was worse than what

I had faced in my early childhood when I was an uncoordinated, retarded kid trying to become normal. Back then I was the "crying baby," and this image had worked for me when I was a child, but no one in America cared about my crying. My teachers could see that my first year of classes at Berkeley was so stressful that the school ended up giving me some financial aid to obtain language tutoring. But no matter what, I had to maintain passing grades or I would be deported back to Korea.

By now I had my own place. I was paying $80 to rent a small room. Because I couldn't afford transportation, I walked for more than an hour from school to home. I'd arrive home around 4:30 P.M., and I'd have to sleep or study before going to my dishwashing job. I was forced to quit my job at the restaurant on Montgomery Street because it was too far from my home and school, so now I worked washing dishes at the local Denny's. From 10 P.M. until 6 A.M. I got everything cleaned up for the breakfast shift.

Except for weekends, I was almost always a walking zombie. When I'd finish work and walk to school, many times I'd bump my head on low-hanging tree branches or narrowly miss getting run over by a car. My eyes were open but not working properly. I was walking on autopilot, and that didn't always work. Sometimes I would walk for a half hour and then discover that I was in the wrong neighborhood. I would then have to backtrack just to get back on schedule.

My shoes couldn't handle the daily two-and-a-half-hour walk followed by hours of work. And I couldn't hitchhike because I didn't know what to say. As far as purchasing necessities was concerned, I could usually pick up a good pair of leather shoes at a garage sale for two dollars, and they would last me about a month, or six weeks if I was lucky. In the mid-'60s, employees could wear only leather shoes at work, as employers didn't allow tennis shoes. Walking and working all the time in those hard leather shoes was tough on my feet.

Around that time, I began to teach martial arts to a few people. With the small amount of extra income, I opened a studio in a slum area of Berkeley. The landlord was a nice guy, so he only charged me $130 per month. This was $50 more than the $80 I had been paying to rent a room, so I put together a small dressing room and bedroom in the back of the studio. The bathroom also served as my kitchen. The hot water went on and off, depending on the state of the plumbing. Although I usually washed up in the bathroom sink, sometimes at midnight I'd open the back door, and with no one watching, take a cold shower with the hose.

Looking back, I don't know how I was able to keep up the schedule that I did. I would finish school at around 2:30 P.M., arrive at the studio an hour later, and sleep until 6:00. Then I would open the studio and teach classes until 9. I would take a mini-shower in my bathroom sink after everyone left and then walk to work at Denny's to begin the 10 P.M. shift. At 6 A.M. I would leave work and go straight to school. I was basically getting about three hours sleep every day if I was lucky. Oh, and somewhere in all this I still had to find time to study.

Keeping clean was an ordeal. I often arrived at school drenched with sweat. I must have smelled really bad because practically everyone avoided me, and some even complained to the teachers. But there was nothing I could do. There just wasn't anywhere else to shower except my tiny bathroom back at the studio. And washing dishes was like sitting in a steam bath for eight hours. Add to that all the walking I did, and one can easily see the problem. Once again, I was back in my childhood in Korea when no one accepted me or even wanted to talk to me.

Finding time to eat wasn't any easier. When I was washing dishes at Denny's, there was rarely time to sit. It was everything I could do just to finish all those dishes by 6 A.M. and head off to school. While the food in the school cafeteria looked good, I couldn't afford it. I ate most of my meals back at the studio, surviving mostly on Top Ramen. One package would usually fill me up if I threw in a handful of vegetables.

While I could skimp on food and showering, there was no way I could cheat sleep. And once I fell off to sleep, that was it. The place could have caught fire, the firefighters could have broken down the door with axes as sirens wailed outside, and I would have slept through it. Many times I would be awakened by my students pounding on the front door of the studio. Even this didn't always work, so we came up with a foolproof alarm clock. I'd tie a rope to my ankle and throw the other end out the bathroom window. Then if I didn't wake up to the pounding on the front door, my students would go around to the back and start yanking on the rope.

My biggest problem with my martial arts studio was making the rent. When I taught my students in Korea, I never asked for money, for it was up to the students to pay when their time came. The money that exchanged hands was considered more as an expression of gratitude than a payment of dues.

The students at my Berkeley studio were charged $15 a month and a $10 initiation fee. Yet all of my students were as poor as I was, and because I never asked for money, most of them didn't pay. They would just forget all about it or would make excuses. And the only real form of discipline I had at my disposal was "mother love," which I could only use when they made mistakes in their training. I couldn't start whacking them with the bamboo stick just because they were late with their dues. Mother love wasn't made to collect money from students.

But whatever it was that I began back in the mid-'60s in that slum of Berkeley must have stuck, because that studio is still in existence today. Almost 40 years later, the door is still open, and its head instructor was one of my very first students.

In 1966, I found that I could no longer handle the long walk to work, and I was having a hard time affording all those pairs of shoes I needed.

There was a guy named James who lived a block away from my studio. He had a '56 Chevrolet convertible for sale. It was a beautiful car, gold with brown trim and lots of shiny chrome. Although the car was ten years old, it didn't have a single dent on it. I really wanted that car, so I asked James how much he wanted for it. He said $250, and I had $280 to spend. I kept asking him about buying the car, but he kept telling me that the car had problems.

"So what?" I replied. "You're the mechanic. You can fix it."

He would nod and walk off, with me trailing behind him. I would point out that the engine ran and all the tires had air, so what was the problem?

"You've gotta fix a lot of things," he said.

"It's okay. I pay you to fix them. I want the car." I was obsessed with the thought of a Korean guy coming to America and having his own car.

Finally, James agreed to sell me the car for $250. I gave him the money, and he handed over the keys.

"You're going to regret it," he said, as I slipped behind the wheel. "You really need to fix some things and do some touching up."

I had no idea what he meant by fixing and touching up—the car ran, and that was good enough for me. The next day I appeared at the Department of Motor Vehicles, barely passed the written test, and was issued a learner's permit. Technically this was not the same as a driver's license in that it required that I have a licensed driver with me whenever I drove.

I slept in that car many nights. I had seen American movies that had guys pulling into drive-in theaters with their girlfriends, so I just had to sleep in the back of that car. But the big thing was that it was a *convertible*. When I drove, I would put one arm on the door and the other on the wheel and let my hair blow in the wind just like the characters I had seen in the movies. I didn't care if the girls noticed me or not.

I was looking forward to driving the car to work, but I never got that far. Within a few days, I found that I could only drive it two blocks before it overheated and the engine quit. I would have to wait a half hour for the engine to cool off, and then I could drive another two blocks. I had found one of the things that James said needed fixing. But the problem didn't matter to me—all that mattered was that I had this car. I washed it every day and spent time polishing it while I was waiting for the engine to cool down.

I never did discover why the car was overheating. One Saturday while taking my series of two-block drives, I accidentally got forced onto a freeway on-ramp. There really was no way out once I had made that turn. I tried to stop, but the drivers in back of me started honking their horns. The next thing I knew I was on the freeway, and nobody was interested in letting me get off. I was scared to death. All I had was a learner's permit and I wasn't that good a driver—yet here I was on the freeway for the first time. I was giving it all I had (which meant that I was cruising at about 30 miles per hour) when I suddenly saw the grill of a huge semi fill my entire rearview mirror and heard the roar of the truck's horn. I kept pushing the accelerator farther and farther to the floor, but the car just kept losing speed. Suddenly steam and smoke started pouring out from under the hood, and the engine died.

Ten minutes later when the police arrived, they were plenty mad. With their red lights flashing, they used their front bumper to push my car to the side of the freeway, then hauled out their ticket book. According to them, it was my fault for driving too slow and causing two miles of freeway traffic to come to a dead stop. They also claimed that I didn't have a driver's license and laughed when I told them that wasn't so—I had a valid learner's permit, even though I was driving the car by myself.

It took me an hour to walk to James's house. I knocked on the door.

"What's up?" he asked, as he swung open the door while holding a can of beer.

"We're having some problems here. Car is stopped on freeway. You told me that little things need fixing. Okay, let's fix little thing."

"What happened?" he asked after taking a swig.

"Car overheated."

"I told you."

"Yeah, but you said 'little thing.' So let's fix it now. I pay you. I still have $30, you know, so let's fix it."

James drove me back to where the car was parked on the side of the freeway. He threw open the hood, took one look at the engine compartment, and then slammed the hood closed. This "little thing" had turned into a very big thing because now the engine was blown and would cost more to fix than the car was worth. I paid my last $30 to have the car towed to the junkyard, where my beautiful convertible and I said our final good-byes.

chapter 8 :::

A Major Turning Point— My World Collapses

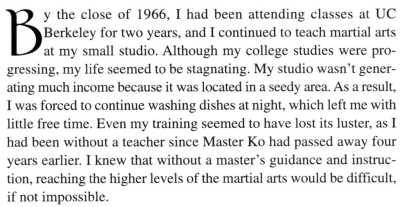

B y the close of 1966, I had been attending classes at UC Berkeley for two years, and I continued to teach martial arts at my small studio. Although my college studies were progressing, my life seemed to be stagnating. My studio wasn't generating much income because it was located in a seedy area. As a result, I was forced to continue washing dishes at night, which left me with little free time. Even my training seemed to have lost its luster, as I had been without a teacher since Master Ko had passed away four years earlier. I knew that without a master's guidance and instruction, reaching the higher levels of the martial arts would be difficult, if not impossible.

Then one day I heard that a Korean master, whom I will call Master K, was teaching in the Sacramento area, which was about an hour's drive from Berkeley. Master K was my senior in the martial arts; in fact, following the death of Master Ko, I had trained with him before I left Korea.

Over the next two years Master K helped me tremendously as a martial artist, giving me both sound advice and opportunity. To this day, I still feel that in many ways I owe this man a great deal, even though, as you will read, our final parting was unpleasant.

In 1967, the martial arts were growing in popularity in the United States thanks to movies and television (especially because of Bruce Lee's role as Kato on *The Green Hornet*). Besides the surge of enrollment in schools, large numbers of martial artists were entering tournaments that many promoters saw as a growing spectator sport. Master K wanted to promote an event that would pit a team of American champions against a team of Korean champions. Everyone thought that such an event would be enormously successful, and it didn't take long for it to come together.

Master K chose me to be captain of the Korean team. So, in order to devote ourselves to our training full time, the other five Korean fighters and I moved to Sacramento and lived in the back of the master's studio. (In my absence, my top student ran my Berkeley studio while I prepared for the championship.) The following year, the American team arrived in Sacramento to fight in the championship. Each fight was to be for three rounds, each round lasting three minutes. Besides a center referee, there would be four judges—each sitting in a corner of the ring—who would score the matches. Although everyone agreed on this point, a major problem arose when neither side could concur on the method of scoring.

During the early tournament years, fighters didn't make contact because many of the strikes in the martial arts are considered deadly. Instead, they would stop their kicks and punches within an inch of hitting their targets. In Korea, at the end of the fight, whichever fighter had scored the most points was declared the winner. This system is identical to the way American boxing matches are scored; however, Americans scored their martial arts matches differently. Instead of fighting straight through each three-minute round, the referee would stop the match each time the judges indicated that a point had been scored, which they did by holding up either a white or red flag. If a majority of the judges agreed, a point was awarded to either the white or red corner, after which both fighters returned to the center of the ring and the fight resumed.

The difference between the two scoring methods all boiled down to a matter of realism. The American fighters argued that in a real setting, a fight between two martial artists wouldn't go beyond the first deadly blow. They likened such an encounter to a shootout in the Old West: If two gunfighters were to square off in the middle of the street, they wouldn't empty their six-shooters into each other and then agree that the gunfighter with the most bullets in him is the loser. In reality, the Americans argued, the first bullet to strike would end the gunfight.

The Koreans didn't agree. The problem with the American fighters' scenario had to do with their definition of "killing blow." According to the Korean team, a punch to the ribs or a kick to the chest weren't necessarily killing blows. Because the Korean fighters were used to taking a lot of punishment in their training, many of them had no problem with placing themselves in a position that would result in their taking a punch in order to counter with three rapid-fire punches and kicks of their own. Although their opponent technically would have scored first, the Korean fighter would ultimately end up with more accumulated points and win the match.

Moreover, the Korean team continually brought up the issue of physical conditioning, for they didn't like the idea that the American team would be allowed to rest every time the match was stopped. Korean fighters were well-trained endurance fighters, and they argued that stopping the match every 30 seconds would amount to a huge advantage for the American team, who didn't train for endurance. The idea that an American fighter didn't have to be in excellent physical condition to be crowned champion also bothered the Korean team.

There was a list of other problems as well, the worst being that the American fighters would be allowed to grab on to the uniform of their opponents and throw them to the floor. The Koreans argued that this was outrageous. That kind of move belonged in judo, and the Koreans hadn't come to fight in a wrestling tournament.

Although the method of scoring should have been worked out long before the night of the championship, it wasn't. Forty minutes after the first match was supposed to have started, both teams were still arguing over the rules. Unfortunately for the Korean team, Master K was forced to acquiesce rather than risk the American team walking out, which would have resulted in Master K and his investors losing a lot of money.

Forced to fight by the American rules, the Korean team took a beating that night. It was such a humiliating experience that when it was over, the Korean team cried together. I don't think I took the loss as hard as the others because I felt that, under the circumstances, I had made a good showing. As far as I was concerned, nobody had beaten me.

Had the tables been reversed and the American team had suffered defeat fighting under the Korean rules, they would have awakened the next day as if nothing had happened. My experience with most American fighters tells me that they tend not to place a high priority on their reputations and their personal dignity. This doesn't mean that they are shallow people, but their main focus is on winning. If they lose today, the humiliation they feel is short-lived because they know they can win tomorrow or next month and be back on top. Maybe Americans are by nature more upbeat and optimistic than Koreans are.

A few days after the tournament, the six members of the Korean team appeared at Master K's office. On one thing we were united—we were going to get our reputation back. Our sole intention was to show the martial arts world that the Korean fighters were not losers. We were all willing to sacrifice whatever it took to restore our dignity.

Master K was all for it. Although he could do little to help any of us financially, he did agree to allow the six of us to continue living in the back of his studio in Sacramento. We sectioned off two apartments that were more like sleeping rooms and survived on bowls of rice and cabbage. In return for teaching all of Master K's classes and handling all his promotional demonstrations, he agreed to pay each of us a salary of five dollars a month.

For the next year, I awoke at 6 A.M. and trained religiously with the other Koreans. Then starting at 10 A.M., I taught private lessons during the day and most of the group classes at night. It was tough going—several

My mother, Oh Ik Sin.

My father, Yu Kwan Kun.

Junior high school, my early teens.

High school,
bundled up
for the cold Korean winter.

Arriving in America—
my passport photo, 1964.

Representing Korea,
winning the 1959 World Martial Arts Championships in Japan.

1971, winning
in Madison
Square Garden.

Demonstrating my aerial kicking on the tournament circuit.

Visualizing "beyond" the bricks!

Most people remember
me by this picture.

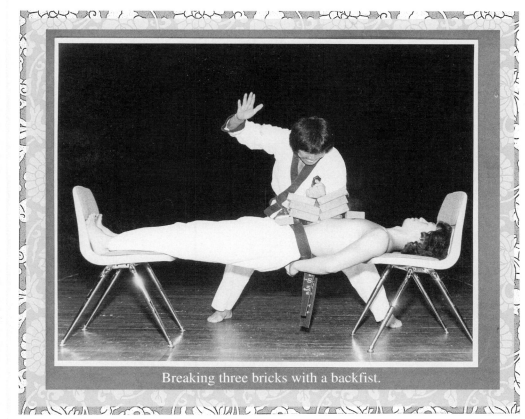

Breaking three bricks with a backfist.

Breaking boards *after* leaping over an obstacle.

Master Ko Soo would have been proud.

San Francisco, mid-1970s—working out with my students in Golden Gate Park.

Clowning around with Muhammad Ali.

From
my
acting
years
in the
1970s.

My
mother's
favorite
picture
of me.

My Ph.D.
graduation
ceremony.

With Denzel Washington.

Still
stretching
at age 68.

With the
incomparable
Stevie
Wonder.

At a charity
fund-raiser
with Pat
Boone.

Left to right:
myself,
Steven Seagal,
Grandmaster
Yamashita,
and
Chuck Norris.

At home
in Southern
California,
February
2003.

of my teammates suffered illness and financial hardship, and it was all I could do to keep the six of us together. But I was determined.

Then one day a telegram arrived for me. It was from a close friend and training partner back in Korea, who told me that his daughter had taken ill and needed to go to the hospital. He asked if there was any way that I could send him $50. I didn't have $50—in fact, I barely had 50 cents. I went to Master K, for he was the only one I knew who could help.

Master K listened to my problem, and then said, "Do you know how much money $50 is? This is big money, and I don't have it."

That was that. I went to one of my students, Jim Prether, who was also a friend. He owned a Denny's franchise in Sacramento, yet he had a big family and was struggling to stay afloat. I didn't tell him why I needed the money, but I asked him for a job washing dishes, which he agreed to give me. After finishing teaching my last group class at 9 P.M., I would have one of the students drop me off at Denny's, where I would wash dishes until 3 A.M. I would then return to Master K's studio, where I would sleep for three hours and then begin training at 6 A.M. After washing dishes for ten straight days, I was able to send my friend the $50 by international money order.

Shortly after that, one of Master K's Korean friends dropped by the studio. This young man had come to America in order to attend college, and was one of a dozen rich kids whose fathers back in Korea were friends with the master. Master K often entertained these young men in style in order to keep up his image. In the course of my conversation with this fellow, he casually mentioned a fabulous dinner that he and his friends had enjoyed the previous night with Master K. "Hey, Master Yu, you should have been at the dinner last night with Master K," he said. "Wow, did we have a feast—New York steaks and all kinds of wild desserts! I'll bet that dinner cost Master K at least $300!"

It always bothered me and the other Koreans who lived in the back of Master K's studio that we were never included on his social list. We felt that we were as good as these high-class rich Koreans he rubbed elbows with. In any case, I didn't believe the guy's story about the master picking up the tab, so I said, "Excuse me, but Master K doesn't have any money."

The young man told me that I was mistaken, and the next day one of the other guests who attended the dinner verified that Master K had indeed paid this lavish bill. I was crushed. The next morning I confronted the master in his office. I reminded him that ten days earlier I had practically begged to borrow $50, and he had told me he was broke.

Master K looked at me with disdain, and said, "These are very important people, and I have to take care of them. But you guys have to take care of the studio."

I didn't understand that line of thinking, so I responded, "Excuse me, sir, what does that mean? I want to know."

He angrily glanced across his desk. "You heard me," he spat. "They are important people. Once in a while I have to take care of them, and that's what I have to do."

I suddenly felt as if the bottom had dropped out from under me. For more than a year I had bitten my tongue and worked as hard as I could for Master K for a salary of five dollars a month and some bowls of rice and cabbage. My friend's daughter was sick and needed to go to a hospital, and this man didn't have $50 to lend me, but had *$300* to spend entertaining the sons of his rich friends in Korea. Granted, I wasn't from the upper class in Korea, but I had been giving Master K everything, while these kids gave him very little.

Over the next few days I got my affairs in order and appeared once again in the master's office. I kneeled down in front of him and said, "Sir, I have to go. I just cannot take it anymore."

Master K was displeased. According to him, I had to stay on and continue working and training at his studio because he had investors that had to be paid back. My sense of duty has always been very strong, so I agreed to meet with his board of directors the next day.

The meeting was distressing. It took place in a public restaurant, yet I was made to kneel down and ask for their forgiveness, in addition to promising to repay all the money that had been invested.

I felt like an indentured servant. Worst of all, in order to ask for my release, I had to kneel before one of my own students, a green belt who happened to be one of Master K's key investors. Suddenly I was no longer "Master Yu," and this student dishonored me by publicly talking down to me. He ended his tongue-lashing by telling me that he wasn't going to grant me permission to leave Master K's studio, plain and simple. (This was the first time I had ever heard this phrase.) But in the end, I was reluctantly granted permission to leave.

I left the restaurant and returned to the studio. After packing my things, I again went to Master K's office, kneeled, and said, "Sir, forgive me—forgive me for everything I did. I will return and pay back every cent you have lost. But please, sir, I ask for your forgiveness."

He didn't say much. He talked about a few things, and then told me I made him sick and kicked me in the face with his shoe, knocking me across the room. He followed this up with several more kicks, then told me that he and his powerful friends would put the gears in motion to have me deported back to Korea first thing in the morning. He didn't have the right to hit me, but he was my senior, so I obeyed 100 percent. He ended his tirade by shouting at me that I was a loser and a quitter and told me to get out.

I walked for the next four hours, heading in the general direction of San Francisco. My face still hurt where the master had kicked me, and I was sobbing uncontrollably. Our parting made no sense to me, nor does it even to this day. I had done everything that I possibly could and had passionately given him my best effort. I wanted to be important in his eyes—I wanted to be like the other guys from Korea who were worthy of a $300 dinner, but in the end I had not even qualified as a friend.

I found myself walking along a farm road. It was beginning to get dark, and I was hungry and thirsty. I ate several potatoes that I discovered growing in a field and later drank several handfuls of water from a trough. I then became horribly ill: Stomach cramps were followed by hours of vomiting—and this went on for two days. I was so sick that I was afraid I was going to die.

I finally did recover, but I had lost considerable weight and was extremely weak. I had to find a way to eat, so eventually I managed to obtain work picking fruit with two dozen Latino migrant workers. I felt like a criminal and worried that the authorities were looking for me with plans to deport me. Hiding out among these fruit pickers brought me some relief. But after a month, I didn't care anymore, so I made my way back to my studio in Berkeley.

When I arrived, some of my students didn't recognize me. Besides being skinny, which changed my face structure, my skin was considerably darker from the long hours picking fruit in the sun. I again had little money, so I went to a thrift store, where I purchased another two-dollar pair of shoes and some secondhand clothes. I moved back into my tiny sleeping quarters at my studio and again began showering in the bathroom sink (with the occasional midnight hose outside in back).

For several weeks I had a hard time sleeping. I was driven to be successful, so I couldn't allow the catastrophe with Master K to ruin my life. I didn't want to be remembered as a quitter and a loser. I was a good martial artist and not afraid to train hard. Years earlier I had promised Master Ko that I would come to America and spread the art. I thought that fighting the Americans in the tournament promoted by Master K would place the Korean martial arts in the limelight. And when that didn't happen, I became willing to train for an entire year for a rematch in the hopes of finally entering the winner's circle. Now that I had left Master K, I realized that I had to become a champion and showcase the Korean martial arts on my own.

Hard training had always been my backbone, and 1969 saw me training nonstop seven days a week. Each day I performed 1,000 kicks because I knew that my kicking ability would lead to winning a championship. Every time I would start to tire, I remembered what had happened at Master K's studio and the last conversation we had before I left. These thoughts restored my energy, and I would train twice as hard for another three or four hours. I was determined to win.

Soon I entered my first tournament. The fighting took place over a weekend, with more than 1,500 contestants and 5,000 spectators. The tournament consisted of elimination rounds, which meant that if I lost one fight, I was gone. In order to win the championship, I would have to win more than a dozen straight fights over a three-day period. I encountered the same problems in this tournament that would haunt me in the next 20 I participated in.

When I fought in Master K's tournament against the American team, I had a group of highly respected Korean masters to argue on my behalf. On my own, however, I was left to fend for myself, and I still didn't have a very good command of the English language, particularly when I got excited. And once again, I was fighting under the American method of scoring.

The biggest problem I had was that as a Korean martial artist, I specialized in jump kicks. When my opponent charged me, I would jump six feet in the air; as he passed under me, I would deliver a kick to his head or upper body. When I landed on my feet, I would look around at the judges, expecting to see four flags raised overhead, indicating a point for me. But no flags were raised. I would ask the referee why I hadn't been awarded a point, and he would tell me that my kick lacked power. The judges insisted on seeing what they termed a "solid base," which meant that I had to have one foot on the ground when I executed the kick. Of course I couldn't jump six feet in the air and still have one foot on the ground!

After hearing that explanation one too many times, I started to make contact with my opponent. I assumed that when the judges saw my kick send my opponent flying from the ring, they could no longer allege that I lacked power. Instead, my new strategy resulted in a new complaint— I had exhibited excessive contact, and they would disqualify me. I just couldn't win.

While the judges weren't thrilled by my aerial kicking, the spectators were. Whenever I fought, the neighboring rings would stop, and everyone would migrate to my ring. When my opponent attacked, I would jump in the air, do two complete spins and hit the guy three or four times from as many angles, and then land solidly on my feet. The crowd would go wild, and many spectators would vehemently object when I either lost on points or was disqualified.

Through thousands of hours of intense repetition in Master Ko's classes, my punches proved to be too fast for the judges to see. When my opponent would attack, I would counter with several blistering punches, then stand to one side and glance at the judges. Again, no flags were up!

I couldn't believe it—I had hit my opponent with enough punches to put him down and keep him down, but the judges claimed that they hadn't seen the punches! After a while, I made a point of taping my hands with bright white tape to catch the judges' eyes. Only then did they start raising their flags overhead to signify points in my favor.

On the tournament circuit, the hard (yang) side of my personality, which had concerned Master Ko many years before, began to overtake me again, and I became known for my hot temper. In fact, I was so vocal that I took on the nickname of "K.K.," which stood for "Korean Killer," and word quickly circulated among the martial arts community not to mess with me or I would finish you off.

Ironically, these same promoters who insisted that my kicks either wouldn't qualify for points or who would disqualify me for excessive contact were the same ones who would come to me during the tournaments and practically beg me to give a demonstration during the awards ceremony.

I performed all sorts of amazing feats: I would leap over 16 guys and shatter boards and tiles on the other end, or I would jump more than seven feet in the air and pulverize a block of ice the size of a small refrigerator with a single kick. As the tournament crew was cleaning up the debris, I would turn to the promoter or the judges and ask them if they thought my kicks had power. They would look at me funny and mumble to themselves. The same kick that sent that block of ice flying in 100 different directions wasn't good enough to be counted as a point two hours earlier when I was fighting!

After I had been competing and giving demonstrations for six months, both the competitors and the spectators agreed that they had never seen anything even close to my aerial kicking ability. Most were actually astonished. Yet when it came to my character and personality, many people began to say among themselves that I was crazy.

Inevitably I proved victorious, for I simply would not be denied. In early 1970, I won the California State Championships, and then went on to win the World Pro/Am Championships. These would be followed by nearly 500 trophies, 28 gold medals, 7 championship belts, and 36 accommodations from kings, queens, and presidents. In subsequent years, I would be awarded three presidential citations (by Presidents Johnson, Nixon, and Clinton) and be inducted into the Hall of Fame as the "Man of the Century" by the Martial Arts Masters' Association. Not bad for someone who started out in life in occupied Korea as a crying baby and Ugly Boy!

In October 1975, I was slated to be the recipient of the Golden Master's Award from the Martial Arts Masters' Association. It was to be the most glorious night of my life. After so much hard work and determination, I was finally going to walk into the limelight. The night of the award, I was in high spirits and superb physical condition. I was truly a champion who brought Tae Kwon Do to the forefront in America. Little did I know at the time that my world was about to come crashing down around me. What was to be my shining glory in fact became the worst day of my life.

The irony was that decades earlier, Master Ko had foreseen it.

chapter 9 :::
Monkey Man

:::

F or many years, the most popular children's story throughout all the Asian countries has been *Monkey,* by Wu Cheng'en. I was six years old when Master Ko first told it to me.

In the beginning, God lived in heaven and had an advisor named Monkey Man, who was also God's servant. When God looked down on the earth, He saw humans and animals, and thought everything was beautiful.

But Monkey Man didn't see Earth this way. When he looked down at humans, he laughed at their stupid mistakes and blamed their stupidity on their lack of intelligence.

One day Monkey Man went traveling in the universe but couldn't find his way back to heaven. Eventually he traveled to Earth, where he observed humans, who fascinated him because the only way they could move from one place to another was on two legs. Since

Monkey Man could fly, he was amazed by all the effort these humans had to expend. Finally, he approached one of the humans.

"Do you know the way back to heaven?" asked Monkey Man.

"Can you see the sun?" the human replied.

"Yes."

"The sun is what created the whole universe and is God's eyes. Just fly to the sun, and you'll be back in heaven."

The Monkey Man was delighted to learn the truth. "I appreciate your helping me find my way back to heaven," he told the human. "Now how can I be of help to you?"

"You owe me nothing," the human said in a humble voice. "I can't take credit for helping you find your way back to heaven."

Monkey Man was touched by the human's honesty and caring. He rewarded the human by giving him intelligence and the gift of fire, and then departed.

A short while after Monkey Man returned to heaven, God looked down on the earth and saw humans intelligently using fire. Concerned, he asked Monkey Man if he knew anything about this, and Monkey Man told God what had happened.

God was furious. He told Monkey Man that he had no right to give away such powerful tools as intelligence and fire. As punishment, God cast Monkey Man from heaven and sent him to Earth to become the servant of human beings.

At the time Master Ko told me this story, I had no idea of how important the character of Monkey Man would play in my life more than three decades later.

Master Ko cherished only one possession: his pet monkey. One of his students had brought it back from Thailand to present to the master as a gift—and he instantly fell in love with it. It wasn't long before the monkey began to follow the master around and even tried to imitate his martial arts movements.

In time, this monkey became a sort of studio mascot, and he would often sit on the floor with us while we ate. While the other students got along with him, I didn't, because he was constantly trying to steal my food. Since I was the clumsy one and not nearly as quick as the others, the monkey would target my fruit and rice cakes. I would be struggling to put the food in my mouth, and *pop!*—he would grab it and take off. With all the other students laughing (and some even cheering), the monkey would then sit just slightly out of reach and eat my food right in front of me. To make matters worse, he would stick his tongue out at me. I took this monkey's ridicule for more than a month. Now and then I threatened to smack him, but he just kept flying around the studio, mocking me.

One day I was alone, eating on the floor of the studio, when he came from out of nowhere, stole my rice cake, and took off running. I had finally had enough, so I ran after him. For whatever reason, on this particular day I wasn't as clumsy as I normally was. When I finally got him cornered, the sight of him taking another bite from my rice cake, which was now covered with his saliva, infuriated me. Without thinking, I struck the monkey on the face with the side of my hand and sent him sprawling into a wall. The sight of him rebounding onto the floor made me feel triumphant, and I still recall thinking, *Great—the little bastard got what he deserved!*

I started to walk away, thinking that the monkey would struggle to his feet and go about his business (albeit nursing a headache for the next hour or so). But he barely moved, and I could tell that he was seriously hurt. I walked over to him and sensed that he was dying. He looked up at me, blinked his eyes a couple of times, and then died with his eyes open, staring right at me. I was scared and didn't know what to do. It was an accident—I truly never meant to harm this animal. But my anger and rage had gotten the better of me. Until the day I die, I will never be able to erase the image of that monkey's face as he released his last breath.

I sat on the floor, held him in my lap, and cried for nearly an hour. I knew I had no right to snuff out another life and found myself thinking back to my beginnings when the doctors had told my parents to put me in a corner and let me die. I had rallied for my own survival because I strongly believed that those doctors didn't have the right to hand me a death sentence. And now I had handed such a sentence to this playfully mischievous monkey, who had done nothing to me but stolen my rice cake.

By far my greatest fear was that I would have to face Master Ko, and I just knew I would be punished with 200 whacks of mother love—or even worse, master love, which was the hardest of the bamboo sticks. By the time the master finished with me, I feared that I wouldn't be able to walk.

Although many of the students had seen me chase this monkey from time to time, there were no witnesses to this day's tragic event. I thought about leaving the monkey lying somewhere or maybe hiding it. I even considered burying him in a grave in back and then suggesting that the monkey had either run away or wandered off. Finally, I settled on just playing dumb. Everyone but Master Ko called me dumb, so this time I figured I would just use it to my advantage. It was the perfect excuse.

I went in search of Master Ko. I had always said good-bye to him before leaving, and I knew that if I didn't, it would cast suspicion on me when he discovered the monkey. I approached the master, who was working in his small garden. The moment I saw him, tears began to stream down my face, because I knew how devastated he would be by the loss of his pet.

Without expression, he asked, "What are you hiding?"

I realized that I had to tell him the truth. Through my sobs, I tried as best as I could to explain what had happened, and that it was an accident. Master Ko never took his eyes off me. He paused for a moment, then quietly said, "Bring the monkey to me."

I walked back into the studio, gently picked up the monkey, and brought him outside. The master took the monkey's lifeless body into his arms and rocked him gently. It was the only time in our many years together that I saw tears fall from his eyes.

After saying good-bye to his treasured pet, Master Ko handed the monkey back to me and said, "You killed him, now you bury him."

I did so. Afterwards, I returned to the master and kneeled down. By this time, I felt terribly guilty, and I told him that I was ready to receive my punishment. Throughout this entire ordeal, Master Ko never so much as raised his voice.

"Give me any punishment you want, sir," I said in the bravest voice I could muster up.

He looked down at me and smiled knowingly. "You have already been punished. And it is a far worse punishment than an entire hour of master love. You have come face-to-face with your own rage, and in so doing took an innocent life. Now for the rest of your life you will have to bear the blood of that monkey on your hands. If you do not learn to discipline and control your anger, that blood will continue to haunt you for the rest of your days. Do not ever forget what you have learned today."

All my life I have battled two weaknesses. The first is that I attack a personal challenge with a vengeance. If someone challenges me to a fight, I cannot refuse. And once the fight begins, I cannot and will not accept being a loser. I must win at all costs.

My second weakness is that if I taste my own blood in my mouth, I go absolutely berserk—I just lose it. When this has happened in my life, I begin to hear the sound of that dying monkey in my head. I hear the high-pitched squeak in that monkey's voice as it was running from me that day at Master Ko's studio. It just gets louder and louder until suddenly I don't see anymore.

These two weaknesses are what led to my being nicknamed the "Korean Killer," who was well known for his hot temper. It turned out that that name was prophetic indeed.

In October of 1975, I was 40 years old and slated to receive the coveted "Golden Master's Award." This award didn't signify that I was the best; instead, it was a recognition of my decades of consistency. Put another way, if I were married to the martial arts, this event was to be our golden anniversary.

I was to be presented the award at the close of the Grand Nationals, which were held in the Midwest. Besides more than 5,000 spectators, scores of prominent martial arts masters were to attend the ceremony. The presentation was to be a highlight of my martial arts career.

Moments before my name was announced as the recipient of the award, a young man stood up in the audience and challenged me to a fight.

This person was neither a loudmouthed heckler nor a drunk—he was a legitimate black belt. He had a laundry list of grievances, most of which had to do with the inside politicking of the martial arts community. This guy felt that he could make his points by attacking my personal integrity and fighting expertise. Several of the ushers and security people tried to calm him, but he wasn't about to get off his soapbox. Ultimately I had no choice but to accept the man's challenge, as my reputation was at stake.

The promoters suggested that we settle the matter civilly, in the ring, rather than end up in an all-out fight in the aisles or out in the street. We agreed to fight six three-minute rounds in which a few rules would apply: Gouging the eyes, attacking the throat, and kicking the groin were disallowed.

By the end of the third round, it was obvious to everyone that I was totally dominating this man. Time after time, I sent him to the ground and hovered over him with my fist poised. Finally he had enough and told the referee that he quit.

That should have been the end of it. But as I walked away, this man suddenly grabbed one of the judges' metal folding chairs and came rushing at me from behind. Before I could react, he had smashed me over the head with the chair—not once, but several times. As I hit the floor, he started kicking me in the head. It took three men to pull this man off me. When I rolled over in an attempt to get my bearings, blood flowed down my face from several deep scalp wounds and ran into my mouth. At that instant, I began to hear the sound of that monkey's high-pitched squealing. To this day, what little knowledge I have of what happened over the next two minutes came from witnesses, who said that I lost all self-control. All I remember is that I truly wanted to kill this person— and when I was finished with him, he was taken away in an ambulance, unconscious.

Although many of the spectators defended me by saying that I had acted in self-defense, none of the masters present would look me in the eye. Instead, they turned away from me and walked off in disgust. It *is* true that I went too far—my actions had gone beyond self-defense.

Moments after my opponent had been taken away, I collapsed to the ground. Only a few of my students came to my side to ask if I was all right. An hour later, I visited this man's hospital room. He was hooked up to all sorts of machines and was still unconscious, and the doctors told me that their biggest concern was a neck injury.

For the first time in my life, I truly prayed to God. If the man was going to die, then I wanted to take his place. What was lying on that hospital bed was clear evidence of my own failure. All the years I had trained for self-control and self-discipline suddenly meant nothing. The man who hours earlier was to receive the Golden Master's Award had unnecessarily inflicted severe bodily injury to another human being. I couldn't stand the dishonor I had brought upon the martial arts community. My knees buckled beneath me, and I fell on that man's hospital bed and sobbed. It was the first time I had ever cried for another human being.

Around midnight, I boarded a red-eye back to San Francisco. I had plenty of time to think about what had happened and why I had found this particular challenge so disturbing. Over the years I had accepted other physical provocations that had resulted in my seriously harming my challenger. But unlike the other times, on this occasion I had lost all control of my art. The thought occurred to me that this was what an alcoholic must feel when confronted with the reality of his disease after his first blackout. In other words, for years the alcoholic drives home drunk and awakens the following morning with a fair knowledge of what had transpired the night before. Then one morning, he wakes up with a totally blank memory—yet his clothing is bloodstained, and the car in the garage is soon discovered to have blood smeared all over the front bumper. At that moment, the alcoholic realizes that his drinking has crossed the line and is now completely out of control.

Two days after arriving back home, I was alone in my studio when I learned that the man lying in that hospital bed back in the Midwest had died. I was devastated. All I could think of was that I wanted to destroy my past—I busted all my trophies, then tore up my promotional certificates and photographs and set fire to them in a metal wastebasket. I grabbed a pair of scissors and cut my hair and ripped out huge clumps of it with my hands. I thought that tearing my hair out would create holes in my scalp that would allow all my hurt and pain to escape. But it didn't happen.

I became deeply depressed, and in early 1976 I turned over my studio to my top instructor and returned to living on the streets. I basically wanted to evaporate, and I never wanted to hear my name mentioned in the same sentence with the word *champion* again—by anyone. Because I associated what I had done with the killing of Master Ko's pet monkey decades earlier, I painted my face up like a monkey and became known among the street people as "Monkey Man."

My life got progressively worse. I tried to kill myself three times, but was unsuccessful. Sleeping became more and more difficult, so I began drinking in order to pass out. It wasn't long before most considered me to be an alcoholic. I drank day and night—consequently, and due to my diet of junk food, I gained 40 pounds. I was sloppy and unattractive, and reminded myself of the "Ugly Boy" of my childhood.

I hung around Pier 39, Golden Gate Park, Chinatown, and Japantown, surviving on panhandling and what I earned from performing street magic and juggling. When I grew tired of the scenery, I managed to scrape together enough money for a Greyhound bus ticket and headed to Southern California, where I hung out along the Venice Beach boardwalk and slept under the Santa Monica pier.

I felt that I was a disgrace to the martial arts, which had been the basis for my existence for as long as I could remember. Without the art, I had nothing. I no longer had a positive image of who and what I was, and I wanted to die. I finally couldn't accept my life any longer, so I decided to return to San Francisco and kill myself by jumping off the Golden Gate Bridge.

On the night I decided to do the deed, the usual cold fog bank was rolling in across the bay. I finished off a pint of whiskey and climbed over the railing. Then I stared down at the water, which looked cold and unfriendly. As I prepared to jump, the last words I wanted to say to the world were from the Korean song "Why Are You Here?" Roughly translated, the lyrics ask, "Why are you here—what are you trying to accomplish and what happened to you?" Those words began to echo in my mind like a chorus of 100 singers.

Then the moment of truth arrived, and I looked down at the water, preparing to leap. But the water didn't look like ocean water. I don't know if it was because I had drunk that whiskey or I had a pre-death hallucination, but the water looked like a huge pool of blood.

An instant later, the face of Master Ko appeared before me, followed by the face of Chung, who was one of my fellow students from that era.

The sight of the master made me recall the hundreds of times I had told him that his wish was my command, and that I was going to travel to America to fulfill his dream. Far below the bridge, I saw tears appear in the image of the master's face, which really hurt me. And when I looked at the face of Chung, he seemed to say, "Your destiny is mine. Go get it, Byong."

In a split second, I stopped myself from falling off the bridge—I came that close to death. I climbed back to safety and broke down in tears. I was so ashamed that I had failed the master, and I asked for his forgiveness. At that moment, I realized what I had first felt while trying to survive the Korean War—that no matter how bad life becomes, it is always better than death.

As I walked back down the Golden Gate Bridge, I kept thinking about what my master had told me over and over again through the years: "Put your life on the line, son. What are you afraid of?" And he was right. Killing myself was the coward's way out. Maybe I tasted death that night. Or maybe I just didn't want to join Master Ko and Chung in that water. I don't think I will ever know for sure.

I found myself thinking of Ronny, an eight-year-old homeless boy I had befriended not long before. Ronny worked the area of Fisherman's Wharf, mainly as a pickpocket, for he had a keen eye and was fast on his feet. Word on the street was that Ronny had been abandoned by his parents, and he did seem to be constantly dodging the police and truant officers. I felt sorry for the boy and allowed him to collect money for my Monkey Man magic act, which included gymnastics and fire-juggling. In return, I gave him a small percentage of the take.

One day I did a really great show, and the two of us had earned enough money for a halfway decent dinner and a couple of ice-cream cones. Ronny felt really proud of the job he had done, coaxing the onlookers to put money into his box. He couldn't wait to show me. "Hey, Monkey Man," he said, "look at this box—it's full of money! When I grow up, I want to be just like you!"

His words hurt me. The foundation of my life had been the discipline of the martial arts, and I had always felt that a daily regime of intense discipline would bring success—yet all it had brought was the death of another human being at my hands. I grabbed $20, gave it to Ronny, and said, "Here's 20 bucks. Just get out of here. Your kind of kid makes me sick. You're supposed to be in school so you can become somebody. You don't know who I am or what I have done. You want to be like me? A street juggler who works his butt off every day to buy a pint of whiskey and a couple hot dogs? All because of money?" I shoved him in the chest and told him to beat it.

He cried and asked, "What did I do wrong? I won't do it again. Please don't be mad at me." He pleaded with me to forgive him and not send him away. But I didn't budge. Finally, he just dropped the money on the ground and walked away.

As I watched him disappear into the crowd, I felt horrible. I had been on the street for more than a year at that point, and I didn't care about anyone . . . including myself. The only thing that was important to me was that I not hurt anyone ever again. I didn't even want to hurt the cockroaches that crawled on me in the flophouses I occasionally stayed in. But now I had hurt this eight-year-old kid, who surely had enough trouble in his life and wanted nothing from me but my friendship.

Even though the thought of Ronny made me sad, as I walked down from the bridge, I was in a great mood, for I had just managed to cheat death. I found my way to Fisherman's Wharf, which was one of my favorite hangouts. I spotted Ronny sitting outside one of the outdoor fish markets. His face was streaked from crying, and he looked miserable. I walked up to him and asked, "Hey, Ronny, how's life been treating you?"

We hadn't seen each other for a month, and he looked surprised to see me. He jumped to his feet and exclaimed, "No, don't hit me!" Ronny had taken a lot of physical abuse, and because I had shoved him the last time we were together, he was scared.

I sat down beside him and slung my arm over his shoulders. "Hey, I'm not going to hit you," I assured him. "And I'm sorry for shoving you the other day. Look, I've been looking for you." I pulled out the two dollars I had left from my pocket. "I don't have that 20 bucks you left behind, 'cause I'm a little short right now. Here's two bucks for a triple-scoop ice-cream cone—how's that for a down payment?"

"I don't want your money."

"Why not?"

"I don't care about money. I thought we were friends."

Ronny had lost much. Both of his parents had walked away from him, and a month earlier I had walked away, too. I knew that his chances of survival on the streets were grim—he would soon become prey for all sorts of horrors, not the least of which was child prostitution. I was determined to reestablish my friendship with this kid. I needed to give him hope.

"Okay, Ronny, here's what I'm going to do. From now on, you and I are partners. Deal?" I stuck out my hand, and he looked at it for a long time, then looked straight into my eyes.

"You don't mean it."

"You're wrong. I mean it more than anything I have ever meant in my life. And that's a promise."

Much to my amazement, he reached over and slapped my hand down. I guess it was a payback for my shoving him a month earlier. I sat there with my mouth hung open, but a moment later he leapt into my arms and began crying, "Okay, Monkey Man, we're partners!"

We ended up sharing that triple-scoop ice cream cone. And as we did, we talked about a great many things, mainly about feelings and about how life can be so scary when you're alone. We both knew what that was like.

Ronny taught me a lesson that night that I have never forgotten, which is that we don't do kids any big favor by sitting around and telling them how great we are. All this does is remind them how far away they are from becoming somebody. What these kids really want to hear is how we got through life's problems, to tell them how we got in a jam and what we did to get out of it. And when it came to sharing these things with Ronny, I had plenty to tell. The more I talked about conquering things like mental retardation, the Korean War, and coming to America penniless and knowing only a dozen words of English, the more this kid wanted to hear. I mean, he became a sponge—as soon as I told him how I conquered one obstacle, he wanted to hear about another. And soon I was able to watch him sleep peacefully through an entire night for the first time. I truly did put a sense of security and hope back into this child's life.

In return, Ronny made me feel human again. Over the many years of becoming a master of martial arts, I had lost the vulnerability that made me a human being. When Ronny first told me that I had hurt his feelings, I had no idea what he was talking about. No one had ever said that to me before. I was "the master"—hugs and feelings and caring about other people's problems were not a part of my character. Master Ko's answer to everything was to be tough, and this was the main characteristic that I incorporated into my nature and taught to my students. To me, everything and everyone in life was a potential opponent. I never displayed kindness to my students, and when they made mistakes, I dealt out mother love, not sympathy and compassion.

After I had been close with Ronny for several weeks, I began to wonder if what I was starting to feel was what normal people felt. While there had been times in my life when I had felt my own emotion, both positive and negative, I rarely reacted to anyone else's unless it was negative. Ronny changed all that—his pure innocence and openness brought emotional balance to my life.

Ronny also put purpose back into my life, and I became willing, if not eager, to put my life on the line for this kid. For the first time in many months, I had a way of paying back the universe for the terrible wrong I had committed at the Golden Master's Award ceremony. I had taken a human life, but now God had given me the opportunity to *save* one. It has been said that God never closes one door without opening another, and I truly believe that.

This chapter in my life ultimately had a happy ending. Ronny and I kept our partnership intact, and over the next several months I helped reunite him with his mother. Today Ronny is 33 years of age, a successful architectural designer who lives in Northern California, with a lovely wife and two beautiful children.

I eventually made my way back to my martial arts studio, even though most of my students barely recognized me. I was 40 pounds overweight, looked shockingly unhealthy, and was coughing blood. I hardly resembled the master who had left nearly two years earlier, but my students were happy to see me. It took hundreds of hours of strenuous workouts for me to recapture the state of robust health that I displayed two years earlier on the night of the Golden Master's Award. But although the journey home had been long and arduous, it felt good to be back.

chapter 10 :::
Master Ko's Wish Fulfilled

•••
•••

After returing to my studio in 1977, I officially retired from competition. I was 42 and had put myself in harm's way for more than a decade, so now I felt that my efforts were better spent teaching future generations of martial artists.

Fifteen years before, Master Ko's last wish had been that I travel to America to spread his beloved art of Tae Kwon Do. Looking back, I feel I have done my best to fulfill my master's dream.

Beginning in 1964, I battled in the trenches, putting on demonstrations and competing in tournaments—39 years later, I am still rigorously practicing and teaching Tae Kwon Do in America. Except for my periods of homelessness, there has not been a single day that I have not worn my martial arts uniform.

I was the first one to introduce Tae Kwon Do techniques on the tournament circuit. Back in the mid-'60s, no one in America had heard of Tae Kwon Do. When I began fighting in tournaments, I put the words TAE KWON DO on the back of my uniform in large letters. There was a humorous side to this—because the Asian custom is to place the family surname in front (in Asian countries, John Smith would be called Smith John), people thought my name was either "Mr. Tae" or "Mr. Do." To further complicate matters, I also put my name on my uniform in small letters. As a result, people would come up to me and ask, "What kind of a name is Tae Kwon Do Byong Yu? It's too long. Why don't you just call yourself Tommy?"

I competed and put on demonstrations in 56 countries outside of America, which led to Tae Kwon Do's being recognized throughout the world as a leading martial art. Due in large part to the groundwork I laid, many Korean instructors were later invited to these countries. In the late '60s and early '70s, a number of great fighters from the east coast of the United States traveled to Korea, where they made a spectacular showing in the Tae Kwon Do championships.

When I first came to this country, we didn't have the World Tae Kwon Do Federation (W.T.F.) or the Kukkiwon (the world headquarters of Tae Kwon Do). I tirelessly labored to build them into the prestigious organizations that they ultimately became.

Due in part to my efforts to spread Tae Kwon Do throughout the world, in 1988 and 1992 Tae Kwon Do was introduced into the Olympics as a demonstration sport. In 2000, it became an official medal sport at the Olympics held in Sydney, Australia—thus making it the second Asian martial art (the first being judo) to become an official Olympic event.

Nothing has had a greater impact in exposing the martial arts to Americans than the media. In the early '70s, due to the enormous success of David Carradine's hit television series *Kung Fu,* the world's audiences were thirsting to see and learn more about the martial arts. Around this same time, my friend Bruce Lee traveled to Hong Kong, where he filmed two low-budget kung-fu movies for Raymond Chow, who was the head of Golden Harvest Studios. When those two movies turned out to be highly successful throughout the Pacific Rim, Chow teamed with Warner Brothers Studios to film what would ultimately become the most successful martial arts movie of all time: *Enter the Dragon.*

Six weeks before the scheduled release of *Enter the Dragon,* Bruce Lee died in Hong Kong on July 20, 1973, leaving Raymond Chow without a star. In October 1972, Bruce had shot some test footage for what was supposed to be his next movie, *Game of Death.* This footage was placed into cold storage at Golden Harvest Studios—yet when Bruce suddenly died, Raymond Chow became determined to make the movie anyway, building upon the limited footage that Bruce had shot. In order to accomplish this, Chow needed someone to double Bruce, so he summoned me to Hong Kong and offered me the role.

For several reasons, mostly creative, I turned down the lead in *Game of Death,* but I did sign with Golden Harvest to do another movie called *The Association.* Although the film did well at the box office in 1974, I was not pleased with my acting performance. So, upon returning to America, I began to study acting at the renowned Actors Studio in New York.

Over the next 15 years, a wave of martial arts movies swept the country. The public interest in the subject soared to new heights, and martial arts schools began springing up by the hundreds. In response to this high demand, I gathered together a group of the best martial artists in America, including weapons expert Eric Lee and the extremely talented Tadashi Yamashita, and became the executive producer of the "Martial Arts Masters Expo." Over the years, we traveled to every major city in the United States, where we put on a spectacular show that featured mass-attack, fighting, weapons, and breaking demonstrations.

It was through these shows that my extraordinary feats of breaking became legendary. Night after night, I would jump across 16 bodies and smash through stationary targets, and shatter with my kick huge blocks of ice that were suspended 12 to 14 feet in the air. Besides sellout appearances the United States, we had successful tours throughout Europe, Mexico, South America, the Pacific Rim, and even the Middle East. And, as a result of my hundreds of worldwide public appearances, I was the guest on numerous television shows, including *The Tonight Show, The Mike Douglas Show, The Merv Griffin Show,* and *Wide World of Sports.*

While over the past three decades Master Jhoon Rhee has been an active spokesman for Tae Kwon Do, and the martial arts have had a number of prominent fighters such as Joe Louis, Bill Wallace, and Chuck Norris, I'm sure that most people remember me as a true pioneer.

In 1995, I was awarded a 9th Degree Black Belt (the highest level in the Korean martial arts) from the World Tae Kwon Do Federation. Due in large part to my persistence and determination to get Tae Kwon Do into the international spotlight, I am proud to say that today it is the most popular martial art in the world. It has taken me much of my adult life, but I now rest assured that I finally did fulfill my master's dying wish. I hope that wherever he is, Master Ko is looking down upon me with a contented smile, knowing that I, indeed, "put [my] life on the line."

Due in large part to my years of training in the martial arts, I have triumphed over the countless obstacles that I have faced in my lifetime. Yet through it all, I have managed to fulfill my destiny and come to intimately discover who and what I am.

Today I have a wonderful life that is filled with loving personal relationships and the deep friendships that eluded me in my childhood. The next part of this book comprises the lessons, wisdom, and tools for success that I have learned along my 68-year journey. May they prove to be as valuable to you as they have been to me.

PART II

Becoming Your Own Greatest Ally

In the Introduction, I mentioned that at an early age I made some crucial discoveries that dramatically changed my life. These discoveries had to do with recognizing that I was born into this life with a specific destiny to fulfill, and that I would accomplish this by overcoming countless obstacles through the use of effective tools gained from years of acquired knowledge. This continuing process of defining and redefining who and what I am has resulted in my own spiritual growth. The material that follows has been structured with this gradual discovery and learning process in mind.

Why Are You Here?

• • •
• • •

A s I mentioned before, at that moment in 1975 when I found myself hanging over the side of the Golden Gate Bridge contemplating suicide, the Korean song "Why Are You Here?" rang in my mind like a resounding gong. The lyrics that asked me what I was trying to accomplish in my life stopped me from jumping, because in that instant I knew that God had never meant my life to end in this way.

When Master Ko told me that his wish was that I travel to America to spread the martial arts, deep inside I felt that he was telling me something that I had known for many years yet couldn't clearly define. This was because martial arts had been my life's passion since the age of six, when I first saw Master Ko walking down the street. I didn't run away from him like the other children— instead, I felt drawn to him. A strange force directed me to the side of his studio, where I climbed on top of that garbage can and peeked through the window. That force was destiny, and it is what I would like to focus on in this chapter.

You Are Unique and Special to the Universe

I remember the day I saw the first televised pictures that were sent back to Earth from the Hubble telescope. They made me feel insignificant. Earth appeared to be about the size of a marble, and I realized that scattered around our small planet were more than six billion people with their own myriad problems. How could God keep track of the universe and still find time to stay on top of *my* personal journey through life? I felt like a speck of dust—perhaps you have felt the same way.

I have an exercise that can illustrate how very much you do stand out, though: Think of someone who is special in your life. By way of example, let's assume that you're a mother with a five-year-old daughter. When your daughter is asleep, walk to her bed and gaze down upon her. Reflect on the reality that if the entire planet's population were paraded in front of that little girl, there is *only one person* whom she will point to and say, "That's my mom!"

That's powerful. And it's beautiful. By the same token, if Earth's entire population was paraded before you, *she is the only one* who you will pick up in your arms and say, "This is my daughter!" Now if *we* can do this with our children, as well as our other loved ones, just imagine how easy this task is for God with regard to His children!

The Hubble telescope only gave us a glimpse of what God sees. You are both special and unique in God's eyes, and I can assure you that if asked, God could easily pick you out a crowd of zillions, and He would know all about your life.

There Is a Definite Purpose to Your Life

The only reason that you are here is to acquire knowledge and wisdom. There is a difference between the two. Knowledge is what you learn, while wisdom is learning how to correctly use the knowledge that you acquire. Wisdom is the ultimate form of knowledge.

The wisdom you acquire over your lifetime is meant to be taken with you into the next world. If this were not the case, then all the lessons you learn throughout your life would be worthless. You may as well just forget about going to work—instead, you should drink and party throughout your waking hours and just wait for death to come.

If you place a high value on people who have wisdom and knowledge, it is because something inside is telling you that learning is most important to being alive. You see this in your children: From the moment they first open their eyes, they thirst for knowledge. They are insatiably curious about the world they suddenly find themselves a part of.

There Is No Such Thing As a Bad Destiny

Some people don't like the idea of a Superior Being giving them a destiny, because they worry that the destiny they've been handed isn't as good as the destinies of others. Even worse, some cringe at the thought of having been given a bad destiny. If you fall into either of these categories, stop worrying.

The universe only seeks good—it does not give out bad destinies. Those people who believed that my fate was to die a lonely death in a corner were mistaken. It was not God's wish that I die of hunger as a child or jump from the Golden Gate Bridge. My mental retardation and physical disabilities were my predetermined obstacles in life. My fate was to conquer them, and in so doing become an accomplished martial artist who would be of great help and service to others.

Knowing that you are unique to the universe and that there is a Superior Being or unseen force of goodness that cares about your well-being makes your journey though life far easier. When you come to know in your heart that you are not walking alone in this life, fear will leave you, and your level of confidence will soar.

Listen to Your Calling

Don't make the mistake of not answering your calling. To do so would be like refusing to open a present left for you under the Christmas tree. There is nothing more pleasing to the universe than for you to win.

It is not necessary for you to win *big*—not everyone is meant to discover the cure for cancer, bring about world peace, or become the next child prodigy. While your purpose in life is connected in part to the whole of the universe, your destiny has far more to do with your own personal growth. Be content in knowing that the purpose of your life is the one you are supposed to have. You are in the right place, at the right time, and with the right destiny. It is one that will add enormous meaning to your life once you put forth the willingness and take the necessary action to fulfill it.

Discover Your Own Destiny

If you are having a difficult time trying to figure out what your destiny is, then you need to reflect on the roads you have traveled in your life so far.

The best way to identify what's important to you is to think about where you willingly spend your time. Reflecting upon this through writing is a good start. Give less importance to what you have *had* to do in life—instead, look for what you have freely and eagerly invested a good block of time in. Place even higher value on areas where you have been driven to invest your time at the cost of personal sacrifice (for instance, if you have survived on a shoestring budget in order to stay in school).

Look back on your life and recall the advice and observations of your close friends and family. If they have been telling you for years that you have a great artistic talent, then there is a reason why everyone keeps telling you this.

And finally, place the greatest importance on what your intuition tells you, for it is often your best source of finding your true purpose in life. Remember, you are not alone in your journey—*that which you are seeking is causing you to seek.*

What to Do If You Find That You're on the Wrong Road

If, in discovering your true purpose in life, you find that you have been traveling down the wrong path, then all you need do is readjust your course. As difficult as making a complete U-turn may be, it is the only way that you will be led back onto a road that will lead you to a happier and more fulfilling life.

Many times in the course of my training with my master, he helped me get back on the right road. The best example is the biggest wrong turn I made in my life when, as a child, I became convinced that there was something drastically wrong with me. I can still recall the day that Master Ko looked at me and said, "There is nothing wrong with you!" You see, I had accepted the claim of everyone else that it would be better for all concerned if I were to die. I had the mind-set that I was incapable of walking, but when the master said those words, I had to accept the fact that I had made a wrong turn in my thinking. Once I had done that, I made the decision to take action and started to train—and ultimately, I overcame my handicaps.

Once you get used to identifying what are usually flashing signposts, you'll become faster at making those U-turns when you've taken the wrong fork in the road. And you'll be surprised at how quickly you can make up for lost time and pick up momentum once you're back on course with the universe. Your depleted levels of power and confidence will be amazingly restored.

Again, nothing is more pleasing to the universe than for you to achieve your life's purpose. God is always watching you. If you become willing to change, and make even the slightest effort, He will put you on the road that will lead you to success.

Expect to Encounter Many Obstacles

Life's obstacles play a major role in helping you learn life's lessons. By far the best way to learn these lessons is through personal experience. While you can read the definition of *honesty* in a dictionary and can learn about it from essays on ethics, nothing will better teach you about the destructive power of dishonesty than having someone personally cheat you out of a lot of money.

Whatever the obstacle, the solution is always contained somewhere in the problem. Just as you wouldn't give a two-year-old child a 10,000-piece jigsaw puzzle to put together, God will never give you a problem that you cannot solve.

Obstacles come in varying degrees. Some pass by almost unnoticed, while others can suddenly come upon you like a tidal wave and send your ship crashing onto the rocks. For example, my ship crashed on the night I was to receive the Golden Master's Award. I was at the height of my martial arts career and living a fantastic life. Then the bottom fell out from under me, and I plunged into what felt like a snake pit. By the end of 18 months of homelessness, I was on the verge of suicide. Although I had no way of foreseeing a positive outcome during this time, in retrospect the lessons I learned over the months when I lived on the streets as Monkey Man were some of the greatest of my life. In the end, not only did I come to a better understanding of who and what I am, but I restored hope to the life of a precious abandoned child.

Life's obstacles can become your greatest treasures, so don't be afraid of them. The most heralded men and women in history are those who have faced and overcome tremendous adversity.

Why Learn All These Lessons?

The reason is simply because the universe is constantly changing. Everything is in a perpetual state of movement; consequently, nothing ever remains the same.

I am not the same martial artist that I was ten years ago, or even last week. Because most martial artists become better over time, I am forced to become more skilled. In turn, this brings me closer and closer to perfection. But if nothing in the martial arts ever changed, I wouldn't have any need to better myself. I would have become a champion and remained a champion. The end result would have been that the martial arts would have ceased to grow, and I would have lost all interest. But that never happened, because I was continually being challenged to reach higher and higher levels.

When I first arrived on the tournament circuit in America, most of the best fighters didn't know how to handle me because they had never had to fight someone with my aerial kicking skill and the speed of my punches. So they had to become better or continue to lose. As their skill increased, I became driven to become even faster, stronger, and smarter. Over the years, each of us kept challenging the other. As a result, I, as well as the martial arts in general, have moved closer to perfection. The entire universe, which includes your life, works in this same manner.

Stay Close to the Truth

There is no greater power on the face of the earth than the pure, unadulterated truth. Famed criminal attorney Gerry Spence is believed to have once said, "We must stick to the truth. When we don't, half-truths soon become whole lies." I totally agree with this statement. Ask any psychiatrist or psychologist what is the greatest obstacle they face with their patients, and they respond that it is getting their patients to tell the truth. Until the patient does this, the therapy is of little value.

This is true in your life as well. Every time you veer from what you know to be the truth, you place another obstacle in your path. While you may get away with misrepresenting the truth to others, you will never get away with lying to yourself. If you aren't willing to live a life based on honesty and truth, then even God can be of little help to you.

No one is perfect, and we all make mistakes and make false statements. What's important is recognizing the wrong you have created and correcting it as soon as possible. Taking responsibility is the only proven medicine, and when you take it, you will again be in accord with the universe that responds most favorably to love, goodness, and truth.

You Will Get What You Deserve

Life is fair and constantly seeks positive results—you do not live in a world that has stacked the deck against you in the hopes of causing you to fail.

What if your purpose in life was to become an accomplished mountain climber, which you would achieve through years of overcoming many dangerous obstacles? And what if as a result of your mountain-climbing expertise, you were able to rescue hundreds of lost or stranded climbers? That's a destiny that could take you a lifetime to achieve, and one that would result in considerable personal growth, as well as your being of great help to countless others.

If this was the purpose God had given to your life, only a mean-spirited or humorous God would then cause you to be born on a tiny island in the middle of the ocean, with not a single mountain in sight and no way of ever leaving.

We don't live in a universe like this. If we follow our dreams, we will surely leave this world a better place than when we arrived. This is the way that all of us help move the universe closer and closer to achieving perfection. By design, we were never meant to come to the end of our life having taken three giant steps backwards.

You will always get exactly what you deserve. No matter what condition you presently find your life to be in, you need to accept the reality that you are exactly where you are supposed to be based on what your performance and attitude have been so far. What you have gained, you deserved. What you have lost, you also deserved. All that matters now is what you're going to do about it.

chapter 12 :::
Blending
East and
West

:::

When I lived in Korea, life was cheap. If someone died, nobody really cared, as there was another body or two coming in to take the dead person's place. Because there was so much hardship and suffering in the country at the time, most people actually looked upon death as a blessing. (This cold view of life was the same in the neighboring countries of Russia and China.) Yet even though we didn't place much value on human existence, as a people we shared a great love for one another in our hearts and were spiritually connected.

When I emigrated to America in 1964, I was excited about coming to the Golden Land of Opportunity, because here every human life has value. Every person has rights, and for the most part everyone respects those rights and honors human life—and property. However, because America places such a high value on the physical world, many Americans remain strangers to themselves and others through-out their entire lives.

Having lived my first 29 years in the East and the remaining 39 in the West, I have learned that both cultures have something positive to offer the other. If you will take the best from both worlds and embrace a way of thinking and living that is based on this premise, I'm sure that you will be pleased by the result. So, in this chapter, I have included a few of my favorite Asian nuggets of wisdom that I think most Americans can greatly benefit from.

Peel the Onion That Is Your Life

A short while after I began attending classes at UC Berkeley, one of my professors asked me what I thought was the key difference between Eastern and Western people. I really didn't know how to express it without running the risk of offending him, so I gave him a hypothetical scenario.

I told him to imagine that he had two students, one who was born and raised in the East and the other born and raised in the West. They're both given the same homework assignment, which is to write an essay on the definition of "Mother Tears," or the teardrops that fall from their mothers' eyes, and both students are given two weeks to complete the assignment. Then I told him how I envisioned the scenario would play out:

> The Western student goes straight to his mother and says, "Hey, Mom, I have a homework assignment. Can you give me some tears in a glass jar?"
>
> The mother gladly gives her son some tears, which he analyzes the following morning in the college chemistry lab. According to his analysis, his mother's teardrops are made up of a little bit of water and a little bit of salt. That's all.
>
> The Western student can't believe that his professor gave him two weeks to write an essay on something so simple. That afternoon he writes his essay, which contains only one sentence:

"The definition of my mother's teardrops is that they are made up of a little bit of water and a little bit of salt." He then heads for the beach.

Two weeks later, the Western student walks into the classroom carrying his single sheet of paper wrapped in a beautiful cover. He looks tan and rested. Then the Eastern student arrives, looking terrible and in need of sleep. His hair is uncombed, his face unshaven.

The Western student hands in his essay, which the professor reads to the class. "The definition of my mother's teardrops is that they are made up of a little bit of water and a little bit of salt." The professor nods, places the essay aside, and asks the Eastern student for his essay.

After nervously clearing his throat, the Eastern student says, "Sir, I could not finish your homework assignment."

"Why is that?" the professor asks.

"How can I define what is in my mother's tears if I don't know what caused them? Are they tears of joy and happiness— or sadness and hurt? Or maybe they're caused by physical pain. Are her teardrops the result of something I did, or maybe didn't do? Is she crying out of concern and caring and love? Or does she weep because of her own childhood memories that happened long before I was born and of which I know nothing? I'm sorry, sir—I just can't describe my mother's tears in two weeks. I probably couldn't do it even if you gave me an entire lifetime."

To Americans, to see is to believe. The primary focus of most people in this country is on the external, or material things. People are judged by the cars they drive, the homes they live in, the clothes they wear, and the company they keep. It also helps to have dozens of certificates and awards hanging on the walls of their office—better still are photographs taken with highly accomplished individuals. If people have all of these visible things in plain view, the assumption is that they are successful people. And if they are successful, then they must be *good*. Why? Because in the Golden Land of Opportunity, where hard work and human life are valued and respected, those who aren't good aren't supposed to be rewarded.

When people who are mainly focused on material things pull into their driveways, they scan what's before their eyes: Does the house look nice? Is the lawn mowed and are the rose bushes pruned? When they walk inside, a dirty home causes them immediate grief, as does an unkempt pet or child.

What a person focused on externals does not do is ignore these superficial signs of well-being and run upstairs to ask Little Jimmy if he is happy today. It is far more important for Jimmy to clean up his room and do his chores and homework. Jimmy gets big smiles for hitting a home run in Little League that afternoon and bringing home a trophy, regardless of whether he wanted to be there or not.

In America, considerable value is put on this external power. Is anyone really surprised when the person down the street who appeared to "have it all" is found hanging from the rafters of their garage?

Asian cultures focus more on internal things. To us, life is like an onion. The first several layers have to do with *love*. The second layers are called *belief*, and the deepest layers we call *truth*. What is in the very center is the *self*. That's you. Even if you have love, belief, and truth, these things are worthless if you don't have the self. You have to have a self in order to experience love, acquire belief, and know truth. A person who is lacking the self is like bamboo: Outside they appear strong and capable, but inside they are hollow and empty. External power is nothing more than an illusion, if *you* are not there.

Cultivate Your Mind Garden

The Eastern way places a far greater value on what we call *mind things* as opposed to physical things. It is of little importance how people dress, what cars they drive, or if they live in an upscale neighborhood. What matters more is what comes out of their mouths and resides in their hearts.

The birthplace of these things is what Asians call the *mind garden*. Only *you* can tend to your garden—nobody else can make you a good and loving person. It is up to you to cultivate self-discipline and self-control and stay focused each and every day. When you do, your garden will be beautiful and flourish.

When you invite someone into your garden, you will want them to see all the beauty that you have created. You won't want them to sit with you and be surrounded by ugly weeds and dead flowers.

The only investment you have in cultivating a beautiful mind garden is your own time and consistency—you don't have to come up with $75,000 to buy a new Mercedes. (And, of course, a beautiful mind garden will last you a lifetime, while the Mercedes will become outdated in a short while.)

Understand Separation vs. Oneness

Americans have always loved to divide things into what's "mine" and what's "yours." When you're moving around in a world based on external power, everything has its own name tag and its own place. When I first came to America, I had a difficult time relating to this attitude. I was especially confounded by how many married couples divide things between "his" and "hers"—each person has their own bank account, their own car, and their own career; and each lives much of their life independent from their spouse.

While Western culture prefers to see things as mine and theirs, the Eastern way is to view everything as "ours." No one is excluded. If there is such a thing as heaven and hell, then we *all* go to either place. In Korea, we make up one family. If something needs to be done, we all labor together. If a neighbor's fence needs mending, we all work on the fence. In the Eastern philosophy, your problem is my problem. I care about you, and I worry about you. If you are sick, then I am sick.

The way to live a more comfortable and rewarding life is to get into the habit of focusing on the needs of others rather than on yourself. For example, the next time you plant a new lawn, make your primary motivation that of beautifying your neighborhood rather than making your grass the best on the block. Plant some flowers in an area of your yard that adds more beauty to your neighbor's driveway than to your own. For one semester let your child's average report card be okay with you. Every now and then, make a point of getting across to your children that having a nice car, luxurious home, designer clothes, and lots of money aren't nearly as important as the lives and living conditions of others. And remember the old adage that actions speak louder than words: Taking the time to eat breakfast with your children in the morning means far more than your calling them from your office or cell phone every day to *tell* them how much you love them.

Know That One of the Best Classrooms
Is at the Feet of an Elderly Person

There is a special kind of wisdom that can be acquired only by living a good many years. When I was a child, my siblings and my parents used to look forward to gathering around after dinner and listening to my grandfather. The things he shared with us about his experiences in life couldn't have been learned from any textbook I ever read in school.

Sometimes people make the mistake of thinking that because someone is old, appears to be growing frail, and perhaps doesn't answer as quickly as before, that he or she has less value. In thinking about this, I am reminded of an open letter that appeared in a Boston newspaper more than 170 years ago. It read:

"John Quincy Adams is well, but the house in which he lives at present is becoming dilapidated. It is tottering on its foundation. Time and the seasons have nearly destroyed it. Its roof is pretty well worn out. Its walls are much shattered and tremble with every wind. I think that John Quincy Adams will have to move out of it soon. But he himself is quite well, quite well.
Signed, John Quincy Adams."

This goes to show that even though President Adams was about to turn 80, he wasn't old—he was just living in an old container. Our elders deserve our honor and courtesy. I for one know that since respect for my elders was instilled in me at an early age, I wasn't just a good soldier during the Korean War—I was a great soldier. The respect that I was taught by Master Ko was carried over to my parents, school teachers, superior officers, and most important, to *me* in the form of self-respect Without the ability to show and command respect, the very foundation of one's life will forever be unstable. That leads me to my next point.

Clearly Define Your Family Relationships

By far the most important human relationships that you will ever have in your life are those with your mother and father. If these two relationships are not in order, then all other parts of your life will suffer. In Korea, the most important aspect of this relationship is respect—not love, *respect*—and it is unconditional. Parents don't have to earn the respect of their children—they are simply given it, *always.* If you are a parent with children who you feel don't show you proper respect, there's a good chance that they learned this from watching you showing less-than-proper respect to your parents.

Not long ago I was teaching a new student, and in the course of the training he casually referred to me as "dude." I became angered, and I can assure you that after my stern lecture and an hour of strenuous training, that student will never again call a 9th-degree black belt in Tae Kwon Do "dude."

Where did this teenage kid get the idea that he could disrespect me in such a way? He got it from years of referring to his father in this manner. In addition, he called his mother by similar street slang, and I later learned that when he was mad at her, he wasn't above calling her a bitch. While this young man refrained from referring to his friends' fathers as "dude," he was in the habit of addressing them by their first names. He'd pass through their living rooms and toss his head back and say, "Hi, Larry," or "Hi, Frank." Not surprisingly, he displayed a similar disrespect toward authority, which is why his parents had brought him to me.

While there is a train of thought in America that it is healthy to become best friends with your children, in the Eastern culture this is unacceptable. In Korea, Mother has a special name; Father has a special name; and Teacher has a special name. You don't call just anyone Mother and Father—that high respect is reserved only for your parents.

Sons and daughters must listen to their parents and obey them 100 percent. Parents are not the enemy. There are no bad mothers, there are only better mothers—in other words, they are *all* good. (It is the same for fathers.)

Also, you can't ask God for another mother or father. The parents that you have are the ones you are supposed to have. In Eastern philosophy, we believe that before this life our children were our bosses. Because of this past relationship, in this life we are now their boss and are obligated as parents to pay them back for all the hard work they previously put out for our benefit. We also believe that in an earlier life our spouses were our enemies. So in this life, instead of hating them, we must love them and care for them. This constant interchanging of roles results in a continual learning process.

First Be Friends with the One You Love

In Asian countries, the divorce rate is less than one percent. Married couples rarely divorce because they are nearly perfectly matched. There are basically two reasons for this. The first is that Asians place a far greater value on the internal makeup (mind garden) of our prospective spouse than we do on their physical attractiveness, possessions, or job. Also, newly married couples in Asian countries are usually virgins. Many don't become involved sexually until months after they are married. Instead, they spend time learning how to live together under the same roof.

The second reason is that the parents of both prospective newlyweds are very much involved in determining whether these two people are properly suited for each other. This makes sense—after all, who better than the parents know the true nature of these people?

In America, the parents of engaged couples are rarely invited to participate to this degree. While they are generally asked if they "approve" of the marriage, the notion of the parents of both children sitting down and thoroughly discussing their knowledge of their children's personalities, strengths, and weaknesses would be viewed by most Western engaged couples as meddling and mistrustful of the intense love they claim to share for each other. Perhaps the high American divorce rate could be improved upon if couples would try the Eastern method of selecting a lifemate by welcoming the thoughts and wisdom of their parents. It's at least worth thinking about.

chapter 13

Being a Part of Rather Than Apart From

• • •
• • •

Coming to know who and what you are is a big accomplishment, but it will be of little value if you feel separated from those around you, the world you live in, and God, Who created you.

Few people could stand the emotional isolation of solitary confinement. Someone once said that "one chimpanzee is no chimpanzee." I believe that's true. This chapter is about our basic human need for other people.

Get in the Game

If you feel an emptiness in your life, chances are that you've been sitting on the sidelines, watching the world from a distance. The only way you're going to fill this void is to become a participant in life rather than stay a spectator.

When I first came to America and lived as a homeless person in San Francisco, I used to perform my martial arts training in Golden Gate Park. I isolated myself from those who showed an interest in what I was doing because I was too proud to let them know that I was hungry and penniless. But as long as I continued to remain in isolation, I would remain a spectator of life. It wasn't until I chose to become a participant and took to cleaning that alley behind the restaurant that my life began to turn around.

A major part of feeling a sense of belonging is knowing that you have a place to go where you're needed. If you don't have that in your life, make it a high priority. Besides making you feel good about yourself, you will bring joy to the lives of others in need. Acts of kindness don't have to be on a grand scale—it is often the little things that bring the most joy.

When I was homeless and scrounging for food in garbage cans, I used to save a portion of whatever I would find for a male cat that hung around Golden Gate Park. This little guy would wait for me, no matter how late I was. He would spot me coming and offer a friendly meow. Sometimes he wasn't even hungry—he just wanted to see me and be reassured that I still cared about him. For a while he was my best friend. Over the years I've done considerable volunteer work for the needy, and I've helped bring comfort to men, women, and children who were having a difficult time in life. And I always remember the face of that cat at Golden Gate Park, and that soft meow that said, "I'm happy to see you."

It is so important to your sense of well-being to have things to do and look forward to. While it is often said that the greatest need in humans is to *be* loved, after nearly 70 years of living, I've come to believe that human beings have a greater need *to* love.

Don't Compare

The easiest way to feel a oneness with everyone around you is to stop comparing yourself to others. Don't be fooled into believing that the grass is greener on the other side of the fence. As long as you choose to be someone who is never content with what you have, then it won't matter what car you drive, where you live, or how much money you have. Why? Because throughout your lifetime there will always be large groups of people who are better (and worse) off than you are.

One day when I was homeless, it occurred to me that compared to most of the people surviving back in Korea, I was still living like a king because I was in America. And while I didn't have a key in my pocket that opened the front door to an actual house, I realized that Golden Gate Park was my home. In fact, the entire city of San Francisco was my home! When I changed my definition of *home* from a roof over my head to a state of mind, my life began to improve.

The only one you need to compare yourself to is *you*. If it helps to motivate yourself by being in competition, then be in competition with yourself. Once you're on a path to achieving a particular goal, you should occasionally ask yourself, "How am I doing today compared to yesterday, a week ago, or even a year ago?"

When I first started studying the martial arts, I did the best that I could in light of all my disabilities, but it never seemed to be good enough for a lot of people. But as long as I kept insisting on comparing myself to all those other students, I was really becoming my own worst enemy.

The master had done his job by teaching me to the best of his ability. Now it was my job to learn what he had shown me to the best of *my* ability, not the other students'. As I continued practicing, I worked harder than anyone else, but I stopped doing it for them—I began to practice for *me*.

Learn to Share in the Joy of Others

When you see a guy walking across a parking lot smiling contentedly, and he slips behind the wheel of a brand-new Porsche, what's your reaction? Do you celebrate the joy he clearly feels in owning that car, or do you think, *What does that guy have that I don't? That son of a bitch, I'll bet I have twice his education. Some people have all the luck. That's probably a leased car, anyway.* If you had a negative reaction, you weren't angry with the car—after all, it's just a couple thousand pounds of glass, metal, plastic, and leather. You were jealous and envious of the car owner's feeling of joy.

Your emotional reactions to the people, places, and things around you are entirely your choice. While you don't own the keys to that Porsche, you *do* have a mind garden, just like the owner of the car. You can choose to plant weeds and spray some poison around your garden, or you can share in that person's joy and cultivate some beautiful flowers that are as good as theirs.

The joy the owner of the car feels and the joy you can feel in celebrating his good fortune *are the same.* Joy is joy. And if you are able to do this, then you need never own a Porsche, a new house, a yacht, or any other material possessions. All you have to do is develop the ability to *share* in the joy, happiness, and good of others rather than focusing on yourself. When you do this, you greatly lessen the number of obstacles in your life—stumbling blocks that you personally create as the result of egoism and at the cost of diminishing your own mind garden.

Steer Clear of Being Judgmental

When referring to yourself or others, throw the word *bad* out of your vocabulary. In its place, use the words *good, better,* and *best.* The word *bad* is better used to describe things like poor weather or a misguided idea. The universe never meant for us to use that word to describe any of its children—God doesn't make junk.

Whenever you define a person as "bad," you put them in a category of people that you want nothing to do with, and in so doing, you alienate yourself from them. Whether you know it or not, you have created an obstacle for yourself, because every time you come in contact with them, you have to find a way of avoiding them or beating them down.

People who do bad things are not bad people—they are only *less good.* On the day that I accidentally killed Master Ko's pet monkey, he didn't tell me that I was a bad person. What he said was that I had done a bad thing. Throughout my training, he repeatedly instilled in me that there wasn't anything bad about me. From my first lesson, everything about me was *good,* and I was to try, to the best of my ability, to become *better,* and ultimately, to become the *best* I could be. Again, the levels of good, better, and best are not used as comparisons to others—only to me.

Know That How You View the World
Can Make an Enormous Difference

These days, sunglasses are very much in vogue—and the tint of the glass is very important. Millions of people begin their day by placing a wide range of colored glass in front of their eyes. They walk around viewing the world through blue-, green-, amber-, gray-, and yes— rose-colored glasses. Depending on what color tint you choose to wear, that's the basic shade you're adding to your world.

You do the same thing with your attitude. You awaken each morning and walk out the front door with a preconceived attitude as to how the world and all its people are going to react to you. Through your experience, you've come to see the world as basically kind or mean, friendly or unfriendly, trustworthy or dishonest, conniving or sincere—a long list of opposites. When you add up both columns, your attitude is either optimistic or pessimistic. The world you walk in is either the enemy or your ally. Like the sunglasses you wear in front of your eyes, you give a general predetermined spin to everything and everyone you encounter, including new situations and, most important, strangers.

Give yourself and everyone you come in contact with the benefit of the doubt and make the decision to walk through life with a positive, optimistic attitude. God's creation is one of goodness and love. To know the truth of this statement, you need look no further than a group of children playing, or a baby who offers you a bubbling smile and eagerly reaches out to shake hands with your nose.

Man's basic nature is to trust and to love. If you will approach every stranger you meet and every situation you encounter with the basic trust and optimism of a child, you will be surprised by the enormous difference in your life and the lives of those around you.

Be Passionate about the Life You've Been Given

I believe that from the beginning I have embraced life with tremendous passion. From the moment I realized that I was being placed in that corner to die, I developed a passion about my life that has remained with me for nearly 70 years.

When I first came to the martial arts, I was struggling to overcome my physical and mental disabilities, and upon seeing the martial arts for the first time, I fell in love. I don't know if the martial arts found me or if I found the martial arts—more than likely, we found each other. As I mentioned earlier, *that which you are seeking is causing you to seek.* I think that my experience with the martial arts is a great example of that phenomenon.

The universe was extremely passionate when it breathed life into you, and it will remain so until your dying breath. Honor God and His creation by living your life to its fullest. Celebrate the life you've been given, because it is a precious gift from a spiritual force that is much greater than you.

Earn Your Way

Today far too many people are looking for the fast buck, the penny stock, or the winning lottery ticket. To me, such flowers have little beauty or scent.

I like doing everything the old-fashioned way, which is to earn it. Unfortunately, much of today's young people see washing dishes and scrubbing pots and pans as beneath their dignity. When I first came to America, I saw those jobs as opportunity.

To feel good about yourself, you have to earn your way in this life. When I was one of the scavengers waiting in back of that restaurant, I sometimes felt sick to my stomach after eating those leftovers because I didn't want to be a human rat looking for a free meal.

Within a week of regularly cleaning up that alley, I was asked to wash dishes for the restaurant. I was given the opportunity to become who and what I am today. But first I had to become willing to put forth my best effort, instead of waiting for someone else to pay my way.

Far too many of America's youth have it too easy. They live like royalty for the first 18 years of their lives (or even more). They don't pay rent or have any obligations, and the only job they have is to attend school, which is mandatory. For the most part, these kids don't even care that their parents have to struggle for nearly two decades to pay for their trouble-free existence.

Recently billionaire Bill Gates addressed a graduating high school class. Among the things he told them that they hadn't learned in school was, "Your school may have done away with winners and losers, but life has not. In some schools they have abolished failing grades and they'll give you as many times as you want to get the right answers. This doesn't bear the slightest resemblance to *anything* in real life."

For many of today's youth, reality hits them square in the face when they enter college, where everything is reversed. In sharp contrast to their teachers in high school, students soon discover that their college professors don't take attendance, and they don't care if students hand in their term papers or if they show up to take midterms and finals. If students fail to perform, they flunk out. If they want to graduate, they have to earn their degrees. It's that simple.

Because this new set of rules is so foreign to them, many students simply drop out. Then they wait 50, 60, 70 years, and wake up one morning to realize that they are nothing but a dead body walking around just waiting for someone to dig them a grave.

The problem is that they were never challenged in their early years, because they never had to earn anything. As a result, they lacked drive and creativity. They spent too many years coming home and playing computer games while their mothers fixed dinner and their fathers handed them a hefty allowance and the keys to a new car—none of which they had earned or deserved.

If you have children, give considerable thought to making them earn their way in life. If you don't, be prepared to support them for the rest or your days or be looked upon as someone who doesn't care about the thought of their offspring living unprepared in a demanding world. Today there are many children still living at home well into their adult years. They have a million and one reasons why life is too tough out there, and far too many parents are unwilling to boot these kids out the front door. That's why I believe that the best birthday present you can give your child when he or she turns 18 is a set of luggage.

Dance with the Enemy

Most people who fight in martial arts tournaments, especially if they're champions, arrive with a wall of armor around them. They strut like somebody who's ready to unleash their wrath. They bear angry looks on their faces. They flex their muscles, pump up their chests, and warm up by throwing deadly kicks and punches at imaginary victims. What they *don't* do is walk into a tournament smiling from ear-to-ear and looking for other fighters to invite into their mind garden.

One weekend I walked into a tournament, and everything in my life was going well. I was in a great mood and didn't feel like putting on all that mental and psychological armor and entering the battle arena. On that particular weekend, the "Killer Korean" had stayed at home. So, for the next two days, instead of physically mowing down my opponents (which I was famous for), I basically danced with them. I took the time to appreciate the good moves they made, and on a few occasions I actually congratulated my opponents on something they had done. Everyone was flabbergasted by what they thought was some form of reverse psychology. But it wasn't trickery—I just didn't feel like being a hardnose that weekend. At the end of the tournament, I walked away with the Grand Championship trophy. I got so involved in how well others were doing and my mind garden flourished to such a degree that my physical skills were greatly enhanced.

Oftentimes, the way to win at life is to simply stop fighting it.

Go Out of Your Way to Help Others Achieve Their Goals, Even If You Don't

I enjoy running. In fact, even at the age of 68, I regularly run ten miles in about an hour and ten minutes. I have a group of friends whom I run with, and we really help each other reach our maximum potential. One of them recently shared with me something that his college track coach often told his runners in this regard. The coach said, "If you can't win, make the one ahead of you break the record."

chapter 14 :::
Life's
Obstacles

• • •
• • •

Your journey through life is comprised of years of confronting a minefield of problems. And these problems place obstacles in your path that continually threaten to thwart your forward progress.

A short while after you were born, you faced your first obstacle in life—hunger. Through several rounds of trial and error, you figured out that the way to get someone to give you nourishment was to start crying. Yet no sooner did you get past that hurdle when another one popped up. When you learned to walk, there were all sorts of new obstacles that appeared; after you mastered them, you encountered still more challenges as you learned how to swim, ride a horse or bicycle, and drive a car. In the process, learning how to successfully navigate your physical body through this maze of obstacles also taught you how to overcome a whole lot of fear.

Upon reaching adulthood, you faced more difficult problems—with your finances, relationships, health, and work. You even came upon some challenges that you had difficulty defining, such as depression. If you're like most people, you've discovered that life is a sea of problems and obstacles, obstacles and problems—ad infinitum. And like the great oceans, you will experience times of calm that sooner or later will be followed by life-threatening riptides and tidal waves the size of skyscrapers. Learning how to overcome obstacles is a natural part of the scheme of life, and it's the theme of this chapter.

Understand Success and Failure

The first thing I would like to say about encountering obstacles is that the act of failing at something doesn't mean that you, personally, are a failure. There is an enormous difference between the goal itself and the effort that you put forth in trying to achieve that goal. You can be highly successful in your effort and yet fail to attain the goal.

While I failed four times to pass the test for my first promotion in martial arts, Master Ko didn't look upon me as a failure because he knew that I had given my best effort. The only time you're a failure is when you don't give everything of yourself to the task at hand or you quit altogether. When this occurs, you recognize that your own worst enemy is within yourself.

Failing at any particular task is simply a matter of your practicing for success. The more failure you endure, the greater the celebration will be when you finally succeed. What a great moment in history it was the day Neil Armstrong took his first step on the lunar surface, because so many thousands of people had been trying for years to get a man on the moon. We had spent so much money and suffered so much disappointment, even the loss of human life—then finally the whole world watched in awe as Armstrong overcame one of the greatest obstacles ever. And a proud America celebrated for weeks.

Your Value in the Business World Can Be Determined by Your Ability to Solve Problems

While we feel comfortable watching athletes or actors power their way though two hours of formidable challenges, our hair stands on end when we discover that the water pipe under our kitchen sink has burst or we've broken a tooth on a hard crust of French bread. Far worse is the onset of sudden chest pains while we're jogging or seeing the red lights from a police car behind us when we know we've had one too many drinks.

The reason that doctors and attorneys are paid such high fees is because they have the expertise to get less skilled people through serious problems they can't handle. That is, if you possess a truly unique talent for overcoming extremely formidable obstacles, you become someone who can practically "name your own price."

When I worked as a dishwasher, I did so for minimum wage, because the only problem the owner faced was getting a steady supply of clean plates to his chef. While I had a service to offer, the task that I completed for him wasn't difficult and could have been accomplished by hundreds of other people for the same minimum pay.

However, when I became a grandmaster and champion fighter in the martial arts, the fee that I could charge for my services increased a hundredfold because I was now offering a service that could save lives. While a man eating in that San Francisco restaurant couldn't care less who washed the plate that was placed in front of him, if he left the restaurant and a mugger put a knife to his throat and demanded his money, I could intercede and save his life, and my value would suddenly skyrocket. If this man subsequently came to me for lessons in martial arts, he would pay me whatever I asked for teaching him the tools that might help him save his own life one day.

By Design, the Universe Constantly Raises the Bar

Working your way through the School of Life often mimics working your way through the educational system. As a child, no sooner had you learned your basic numbers than your teacher wanted you to add and subtract them. When upon conquering long division you thought you had reached the pinnacle of mathematics, your teacher handed you an algebra book.

At the age of five, all I wanted in life was to learn how to stand and walk without falling over. Yet just a few years after I accomplished this, I found myself on the martial arts tournament circuit facing dozens of fierce opponents who had the capability of tearing my head off. And when I became a champion worthy of receiving the Golden Master's Award, I was confronted by a man who tried to kill me, and I wound up killing *him.* When this problem ultimately turned my life upside down, I ended up wanting to kill *myself!* But I survived it all and came out the other side a much wiser person.

I often meet people who, when faced by what they feel are overwhelming obstacles in their lives, ask things like, "Who says I needed this?" or "Why me?" My answer to these people is quite simply, "The universe seems to think you did," and "Why *not* you?"

We trust our children with increasingly difficult problems in life so that they will become equipped to help themselves and others. God doesn't treat His children any differently. Welcome the bar being raised in the level of difficulty life presents you—it is a clear recognition that God values your continual spiritual growth and loves you.

The Solution Is a Part of the Problem

Life's obstacles come in varying degrees. Most will be minor speed bumps, while others will be extremely challenging roadblocks. Yet at the same time, the solution to every one of your problems resides within you. The universe will never give you anything you can't handle, because from your first breath of life, God gave you everything you need to overcome any obstacle you will ever face.

If you've been having difficulty overcoming the hurdles in your life, chances are you haven't recognized the solutions. You only have to start paying attention to the clearly marked signposts that direct you to simply ask, look, listen, and trust.

When I stopped myself from jumping off of the Golden Gate Bridge, I came face-to-face with the solution an hour later when I was reunited with Ronny. Of course, the solution to my problem was to stop focusing on my own problems and begin concentrating on the ones faced by this abandoned child, which were far worse. The universe had presented me with this solution weeks earlier, only I hadn't recognized it. This time, I paid attention, and the outcome was wonderful for both of us.

The Key to Conquering Your Obstacles Is Persistence

Over the years of my martial arts training, I have faced countless obstacles. One of the biggest came early in my training when one day Master Ko placed a solid red brick on top of two vertical cinder blocks and asked, "Who in class believes that they have the strength and concentration to break this brick?"

We were all shocked, and everyone but me looked down at the mats, not wanting to make eye contact with the master. After a few moments, I realized that he was looking right at me, and the words *My master's wish is my command* echoed in my mind. I stepped forward and said, "Yes, sir, I am the one who is going to do it."

He smiled and replied, "Okay, son, try it."

I walked up to the brick and looked down at it. Two things concerned me: (1) Was my hand physically strong enough to break through that obstacle? and (2) Was my punch powerful enough? If the answer to either of those questions was no, then I wouldn't be able to break that brick. After concluding that my left hand was strong enough and its punch had enough force, I positioned myself over the brick. I focused on the target for a while, and then I unleashed my punch with a loud yell. But an instant before making contact with the brick, I hesitated ever so slightly. It was enough to spell defeat.

My hand slammed into that brick, sending pain shooting up my arm and into my shoulder. I could hear the sympathetic groans of the other students and saw many of their faces cringe. The brick remained intact.

I had a choice. I could admit defeat and return to the class lineup, or I could make another try. Master Ko just stood there, staring at me without expression. I shook off the pain and hovered over the brick for my second try. I hit it with what I thought was everything I had, and my hand felt like I had hit a bank vault. All that toppled to the ground was a little red dust. My hand was throbbing. I thought about trying again with my other hand, but I knew that my right punch wasn't as powerful as my left.

I decided to make one final attempt, knowing that either my hand or that brick was going to break. I pulled out all the stops, focused intently, and slammed into that brick like a pile driver. The brick shattered into four pieces and fell to the floor.

That incident took place more than 50 years ago—in the years to follow, I gradually increased the number of bricks that I could break, reaching a maximum of seven. Most grown men can't accomplish that feat, even with a 40-pound sledgehammer.

It's true that an expert is simply a beginner who never quit. This is as true in life as it is in the martial arts. Whatever your dreams, all you need to achieve them is to simply not give up—no matter what. If the dream you have is important enough to you, then its fulfillment is equally important to the universe. This next point clearly illustrates that.

Embrace a Positive Mind-set

When I first started fighting in tournaments in Korea, I lost my first 26 matches. I couldn't believe the scale of my defeat—*26* matches in a row! The main reason I lost was because I never thought I could win. Losing the match never hurt because I already expected to lose, even though I knew that I had given my best physical effort. And I never quit.

Then one day Master Ko told me, "If you do not want to lose, then act, think, and train like a champion." The easiest part was training like a champion, for all I had to do was watch how they trained and then model what they were doing. The most difficult obstacle here was to teach myself to think and act like a champion *before* I actually became one.

Those who become champions truly believe in their capabilities. And the master had given me this. He told me constantly that I could win a championship if *I* honestly believed that I could win. He assured me that a constant regime of focused training would result in my having the necessary tools. He already knew from the first day that I had both the heart and spirit, and he kept telling me, "Put your life on the line, son." As to acting like a champion, I knew that I had the one, if not only, requirement for having a positive mind-set, and that was to promise myself that no matter what, *I would not quit!*

Let Hardship Work in Your Favor

Hardship has always been the backbone of my life, and it's what has often driven me to the point of exhaustion. Often you will find that you put forth your best effort when your back is against the wall—in other words, the best time to learn how to swim is when you're drowning. Why? Because you have nothing else on your mind to distract you.

Over the years, I have watched many people become complacent after they've experienced a fair degree of success. They get a little money in the bank, and soon they start thinking about slowing down, taking a vacation, or even retiring.

During my lifetime, I have fallen into that trap several times. When this happens, I often restore my motivation by spending a day or two with the homeless. I go back and live on the streets, and I remember how life was when I didn't have choices. Today I am a very fortunate man—I have a place to work and a home where I can eat and sleep. I can change my clothes every day, and all of my apparel is clean. It wasn't always that way. So I find that returning to the slums restores my drive.

If you find yourself worrying that you are becoming complacent, return to the time and place in your life when things weren't nearly as good as they are for you today. Return to your old neighborhood, or thumb through your high school yearbook, or spend a few hours looking at old childhood photographs of yourself and your environment when times were tough. Recall all the hard work you've gone though in order to achieve what you have today. It will be time well spent.

Be a Smart and Compassionate General

Don't waste time and energy prolonging battles that you've already won. When you're involved in a confrontation with another person, don't continue to beat on them long after you've clearly won the battle. This is a lesson I had to learn when that man challenged me on the night of the Golden Master's Award. I didn't have to fight him. I knew I had the fighting expertise to beat him, even if *he* didn't.

There are some battles in life that are either the wrong ones or ones you need not fight at all. You would be wise to develop the ability to clearly identify such unnecessary confrontations. Following is an example of what I mean.

About a year after I began my martial arts training, I forgot that the art is for self-defense, not offense. Somehow I got the idea that hunting would be a great way to display my power, and I managed to get my hands on a pellet gun. A group of us headed into the mountains in search of animals we could shoot. We set out to be big-game hunters that day. We got about halfway up the mountain when I spotted a rabbit. It saw me at the same time and took off running. I aimed and shot at it, and it fell to the ground. I was delighted and felt like a big trophy hunter. I started yelling excitedly, "I got him! I got him!"

I ran over to this fallen rabbit, and when I looked down at it, I was horrified. The pellet had hit its leg, which was now all bloody and twitching. That animal looked up at me with a look of true desperation. I dropped that pellet gun on the ground and said to the others, "I did a terrible thing. I thought it would be a joy to hunt, that it was just sports, but it's not. I'm going to be sick." The memory of that day still troubles me. From that moment on, I have never aimed a gun at an innocent animal.

People who can't defend themselves can't give you a fair fight—either physically, in business, or during a personal argument—and it's better that you leave well enough alone. If you don't, then you are nothing more than a bully. You become the person who pushed Humpty Dumpty off the wall and got pleasure from watching him fall to the ground and break apart in pieces. There is never any honor in being a bully, and you will only diminish your self-respect and the esteem of others.

Only Confront Obstacles That Are Personal in Nature

"Road rage" is often in the news today. People have been needlessly killed in traffic accidents and even shot to death as a result of minor, and usually inadvertent, errors in driving.

Imagine that you're motoring down the freeway and accidentally cut in front of another car. As a result, the other driver blares his horn at you, shakes his fist, and makes an obscene gesture. Is his reaction personal, or does it have absolutely nothing to do with you? If you take it personally, your reaction is, "Who the hell does this jerk think he is? Doesn't he know who *I am?*" The answer is no. He has no idea who you are—he doesn't know your name or the names of your children, what you do for a living, or anything else about you. If the two of you are pulled over to the side of the road by the highway patrol, the driver of the other car will refer to you as "that damn idiot in the blue Trans Am!" or "the driver of the white BMW!" From the start of the confrontation, he has never had a sense of you *personally.*

You will save yourself a lot of heartache in your life if, when confronted by another person, you'll take a few seconds to ask yourself, "Is this person getting upset with me because of something personal, or am I just the object of some other problem that has absolutely nothing to do with me?"

Other people are simply a mirror of you, and you are a mirror of them. You can't dislike something about another person or their actions unless it reflects something you dislike about yourself. When tempted to criticize others or lash out against them, ask yourself why you feel so strongly. When someone lashes out at you, ask yourself if the problem has to do with something about *you* or something inside *them.* If the problem has nothing to do with you, then walk away.

The Ways to Conquer Life's Obstacles

When all is said and done, I know of only three ways to respond to life's obstacles:

1. Walk away. Master Ko often said, "When trouble comes, do not be there." By this, the master was referring to those problems that just aren't worth your time and effort, or obstacles that will end in a negative result for all concerned. Don't fight a battle that can't be won by anyone. An obnoxious drunk in a bar or someone challenging you to drag-race on the freeway are not worthy of your effort.

2. Go around them. When a river running down a mountainside encounters a tree, it easily goes around the tree rather than attempting to plow through it. Many great battles have been won by generals ordering their troops to go around the enemy and attack their flank. If you're confronted by an 800-pound grizzly bear in the forest, you would be wise to quietly go around it. I defeated a good number of my opponents in my championship fights by moving to the side or above them as they launched their straight-line attack. I scored points as they tried to pass through me, as I was no longer there.

3. Conquer them. Because of the specific way that I was trained in the Korean martial arts, I have a strong preference for conquering the obstacles I've been presented in life by facing them head-on and going straight through them. This is best illustrated by the breaking of bricks, which represent obstacles. A brick has a front, middle, and back; but most important, it has a "beyond," which represents the end result of a problem.

When I break through a stack of bricks, I don't aim at the bricks themselves. I aim beyond them, because that's where the end result is located. In order to break through those bricks, my fist has to end up in the *beyond,* so that's my target reference. If I don't punch through to the beyond, I will never break the bricks; the bricks will break my hand.

Life's obstacles are identical to a stack of bricks in that they have a beginning, middle, and end. If you firmly believe that the obstacle can't stop you and that you have enough strength and wherewithal to get though it, then you've already won the battle. All you need to do is commit yourself 100 percent, focus, believe that you can achieve the result you want, and then follow through. You will persevere.

chapter 15 :::
Tools and Winning Combinations

:::

We occasionally hear about people wanting to freeze their bodies in liquid nitrogen so that they can be thawed out sometime in the future. Others look into their past lives in the hope of understanding what's going on with them today (and talking to the dead has become popular in the past few years as well). Then there are all those millions of people who are convinced that their lives will begin when they get to heaven.

I often meet people who are searching for the great teachers. They've spent years trying to connect with the wise sages, maestros, and turbaned gurus sitting cross-legged in the desert or on a mountaintop. While these people can be of some help in guiding you along your journey, the truth is that the greatest teacher you have is . . . you.

No one knows you better than you know yourself. Only you know what's really preventing you from becoming a better person each minute of every day. You know where all your roadblocks are, and you'll be the first to spot the signposts, red flags, and storms brewing on the horizon. Instead of being your own worst enemy, become your best ally.

During my childhood in Korea, I placed many roadblocks in my life that caused inappropriate knee-jerk reactions not long after I arrived in America. Upon becoming homeless, I again began to see myself as "Ugly Boy." I felt helpless and shied away from making friends because deep inside I felt that no one liked me. I needed to realize that I didn't arrive in America as a human rat—I came to this country as an educated man and a martial arts champion. As a result, within days I landed a job and found a good friend in Vicky, the waitress who saw the goodness in me—goodness that I no longer saw in myself because of old hurdles that had suddenly reappeared in my life and stopped my forward progress.

Chances are you have similar challenges in your life that are no longer appropriate. Dig up those old mines and defuse them. In most cases, the enemy has long since departed. Why leave those explosives for those who aren't your enemies or, worst of all, accidentally step on one of those mines yourself? As Master Ko often told me, "Trust in yourself. You have nothing to be afraid of."

I have no interest in past lives, crystal balls, the afterlife, or talking to ghosts. My focus is on the here-and-now, for I believe that heaven is right here on earth. These days, my main concern is to become a better human being and live a long, healthy life. What follows are the tools that have served me well for many decades.

Four Basic Elements Needed for Survival

In order to survive an actual physical attack, an effective martial artist needs four basic elements: (1) knowledge, (2) accuracy, (3) timing, and (4) power. Master Ko taught these elements to me 40 years ago, and I teach them to my students today. Besides being effective against a physical street attack, these same basic elements are extremely practical when dealing with life itself. In a strange way, it's almost as if the martial arts imitate life, or maybe life imitates the martial arts. I teach the following principles in my seminars to martial artists and non-martial artists alike, and they have worked wonders in many people's lives.

1. Knowledge

The first principle that you need is *knowledge*. Without understanding just how your environment operates, you won't last long. Some knowledge you're born with (such as knowing not to breathe underwater), but most you've learned from either personal experience or a teacher.

I define *knowledge* as everything that you have stored in your brain. Getting rid of old, misguided knowledge is just as important as obtaining new, correct knowledge. What follows are some techniques that will help you in this area.

Attend Your Own Funeral

Anyone who works with a computer knows the importance of routinely deleting files and folders that are no longer useful in order to make the machine run more efficiently. If you don't clean, scan, and defragment the hard drive, it can lock up or even crash.

Women perform a similar cleaning with their purses. Every now and then, they dump the entire contents on a table, put back in those things that are useful, and then discard the rest. By the same token, if you want to keep your *mind* running efficiently, you should occasionally empty it, reorganize it, and then, as with a computer, reboot it.

In the late 1960s when I had my studio in Berkeley, one of my students was a juvenile court judge. One day he asked me to come to the courthouse and join him in his chambers. He was dealing with a kid who was well on the road to becoming a habitual criminal, so he asked if I would be willing to take the boy under my wing. The judge had seen firsthand the positive results of martial arts training and wanted to include such discipline as one of the conditions of this kid's probation. I agreed to give it a try.

The following Monday this kid arrived for lessons, and by the end of two weeks, he was testing my boundaries every chance he got. He arrived late and wanted to leave early. Several times he showed up without his uniform and wanted to know what was wrong with training in jeans and a T-shirt. And he had a mouth that wouldn't quit.

By the end of the third week, I'd had enough. When he arrived for his lesson, I told him to forget about suiting up—instead, he should follow me out back. There was a vacant lot behind my studio, and I walked this boy to the middle of the field and pointed to a pick and shovel I had placed on the ground.

"Your training today is you're going to dig!" I said.

The kid looked at me with defiance and retorted, "Dig what?"

"A hole. Eight feet long, four feet wide, and six feet deep!" I barked back.

The boy was aghast. "You want me to dig a grave?"

"That's right. If you refuse, I'll call the judge right now, and he can send a police unit over here to drive you to that detention center. I have had it with you."

The boy argued with me for a few minutes but finally gave in. It took him nearly two hours in the hot sun to dig that hole, and when he was finished, I reappeared.

"Get in!" I said, pointing down at the bottom.

"What, are you crazy? I dug the hole like you said."

"What I said was 'get in'! Lie down on the bottom—on your back with your eyes looking straight up!"

Reluctantly, the kid did as he was told, for he knew I meant business. After clearing away some rocks, he lay down on his back with his arms at his sides.

"I'll be back in an hour," I informed him. "And I'll be checking in on you every now and then, so just stay in that position and don't even think about going to sleep!"

The kid seemed relieved that I wasn't going to start shoveling dirt on top of him. I did check on him several times, and at the end of the hour I peered down on him. His eyes were bulging, his face was ghostly white, and his body was drenched in sweat. It was hot down at the bottom of that hole, but the sweat that covered him was caused by fear.

"All right, climb out of there!" I ordered in a firm voice.

The boy scrambled from that hole like he was being chased by a great white shark. He dusted himself off, wiped the sweat from his face, and then stood staring back at me.

"How was it down there?" I asked.

"Horrible. I'm glad I'm out," he replied in a weak voice.

"I'm sure you are. Now I'm going to tell you something. You keep leading the life you've been living—hanging out with those gangs and running off that mouth of yours and disrespecting your parents, teachers, and every other authority figure in your life—you'll be back in that hole a lot sooner than you think. Only on the next trip, your eyes won't be open, and you won't be breathing because you'll be dead. Do you understand what I'm saying?"

"Yes, sir," he replied.

It was the first time I'd heard him speak sincerely. I could tell that he was scared—he had tasted what it would feel like to die an early death, and he wanted no part of it.

"All right," I responded. "Come back into the studio. You're not finished with today's lesson."

"Yes, sir."

He followed me into the studio, where I sat him down and handed him a tablet of paper and a pen.

"I want you to write down all the things you don't like about yourself. Write about that defiant attitude you have, about the things you've done in your life that you're not proud of, and your unkind thoughts. If you'd like to see me dead because I put you in that hole, write that down. I'll be back in an hour, and I want to see those pages full."

"Yes, sir."

That kid worked hard for the full hour. In fact, he became so engrossed in what he was writing that he asked for an additional 15 minutes. Finally, he appeared at the doorway to my office and told me that he was finished. He handed me the tablet, expecting me to read what he had written.

"I don't want to read it," I said. "And no one else is going to read it either. Follow me."

We walked back to the hole he'd dug in back of the studio. I pointed at the bottom and said, "Throw it in."

After he threw the tablet into that grave, I told him to take the shovel and fill up the hole. Fifteen minutes later the job was finished.

This time I talked to him in a much softer voice: "What you've done today is to tend to your mind garden. You've cleaned up a big mess that was in there and buried it forever. All those things that you didn't like about yourself are no longer a part of your garden. They're buried and gone."

For the first time in years, that kid heard something that made him feel good about himself. He fell into my arms and broke down in tears. After he had a good and long-overdue cry, we returned to the studio because he wanted to resume his training. He took a quick shower and put his uniform on. Those next two hours with him were some of the best I've ever spent with a student—that kid gave me his all, and he was proud of his accomplishments.

Over the next six months, I intensified his training. The change in him was miraculous. Ultimately, he completed his probation without incident and graduated from high school with good grades. Years later, he married and fathered two fine children. I often hear from him, and he tells me that his life just gets better and better—and it all began from the day he emptied his mind and buried the parts of himself that were preventing him from becoming the best person he could be.

You can do a similar exercise that will empty your mind of all the negative thinking that's causing you to be your own worst enemy. Set aside a few hours and go to a quiet place where you won't be disturbed. Take a tablet of paper and pen and write down all the things you don't like about yourself. Be sure to include the times in your life where you have done or said things that have been hurtful to others. When you've finished, find a place to bury that tablet. You don't have to dig an actual six-foot grave (unless you want to)—you can throw that tablet into the bottom of your garbage to be taken to the local landfill. What's important is that, from the moment you discard that tablet, you walk away from it with the conviction that you have buried the negative side of your old self forever and that it will not be returning. If you've done this with sincerity and honesty, I guarantee you that you'll be amazed by how good you'll begin to feel about yourself and the world around you.

Place a Guard at the Entrance to Your Mind Garden

Now that you've rid your mind garden of ugly weeds, it's important that you post a guard at the entrance. You need to start being aware of the seeds that you allow to be planted in your garden—if you want to grow beautiful plants and flowers, then only let positive seeds come in. Just as one rotten apple will eventually spoil the entire barrel, if you allow negative seeds to be planted, you'll end up growing weeds that will eventually overrun your garden.

Negativity comes in many forms, so start paying attention to the books you read, the people you let give you advice and information, the television programs you watch, and the songs you sing. Most important, seek wisdom and counsel from the elderly members of your family.

The choice is always yours. Choose to allow only positive influences into your life and you can rest assured that your mind garden will flourish. If the guard you've placed at the entrance to your mind is loyal, dependable, and vigilant, then you'll find that more and more people—everyone from loved ones to strangers—will want to come into your garden to sit with you.

Accept That the Moment You Decide to Stop Learning Is the Moment You Begin the Dying Process

On the day of my graduation from the sixth grade, the entire school was in attendance. Most of the students were surprised to learn that I was on the list of those receiving an accommodation or special award. Yet, after many of the other students were given their accommodations, which were mainly for scholastic achievement, I was called to the stage to receive mine. I was the only student to receive this award, and many felt that it was the most difficult of all: *I had not missed a single day of school for the entire six years—not one day.* Even with all the hardship and ridicule that I had endured, my enthusiasm for school had never waned, and I was always grateful that standing in the front of the classroom was a teacher whose main goal was to help me become a better person.

Throughout my life I've placed a high value on learning. Besides formal education, I've continually sought the teachings of individuals who have gained wisdom from years of living. That you have chosen to take the time to read this book is a good indication that you feel the same way. As long as you continue to learn, you'll continue to grow. When you choose to stop learning, you bring a halt to the growing process and send a signal to your body and spirit that you're approaching the end of your journey.

2. Accuracy

The second quality that's important for survival is *accuracy*. You have to be able to coordinate your knowledge so that when presented with a set of challenging circumstances, you can come up with the right response. For example, if you knew that a heavy object falling on you could crush you to death, and you were faced with the sound of a tree cracking and the sight of a 100-footer falling toward you, then the accurate response would be to run like hell.

While on the surface this may appear to be a simple matter of common sense, you'd be amazed by how many people I've seen misuse their knowledge. I'm no exception—I misused my knowledge of the martial arts when I shot that defenseless rabbit, tried to force violent tactics on those nonviolent villagers, and killed that man the night I was to receive the Golden Master's Award.

In martial arts, *accuracy* means that the student must become skilled at effectively hitting the targets, while at the same time intercepting or misdirecting the incoming weapons before they strike. The principles I use to perfect accuracy in my art are the same ones you can use to perfect accuracy in your life.

Remember: If You Train Hard and
Don't Quit, You Can Win

If you're a painter and you want to become the best, then you must keep painting and painting and painting until you reach your highest level of accuracy. The same thing applies to any job in life. What you can't do—ever—is quit! That is the one word that I refuse to hear from my students or myself. In 68 years, I have never quit. I don't accept quitting, no matter what. If you can keep this eleventh commandment—"Thou Shalt Not Give Up"—then you can win at anything in your life that you commit your mind and body to.

Harness Your Mind-set As You Strive for Perfection

From the beginning of my training, Master Ko constantly made me strive for perfection. This often frustrated me because with all my disabilities, I was convinced that a goal of becoming a perfect martial artist was unreachable.

Years later, I realized that I had misunderstood the master. It wasn't the goal of perfection he was after, but rather the *mind-set* of perfection. In other words, crossing the finish line of a race is not nearly as important as *driving* for the finish line, to know the *feeling* of striving for that outstretched tape with everything you've got.

Most people I've met never strive for perfection in any area of their lives because they don't think they have anything to offer that's worth perfecting. What they fail to recognize is that it isn't the result that matters, but the process—that's what makes the experience so worthwhile and exhilarating.

You don't have to invent a better mousetrap or discover the cure for cancer in order to feel alive and give life your best. For example, last year one of my students arrived at the studio and showed me a sheet of paper that he had printed from an Internet Website. It was a list of the "top ten hamburgers in Los Angeles." This guy liked to eat, and he had made plans with a group of his friends to visit all ten of these places to see just how good these burgers really were.

Throughout his training, I had a hard time getting this guy to put forth his best effort. He never thought his best was good enough, and he had a fear of failing. So I asked, "Why don't you guys forget those places and spend an afternoon *creating* the perfect hamburger?"

"None of us are that good a cook," he replied.

"You don't have to cook anything but the meat, right?"

"I suppose so," he said with a glimmer of interest.

"In fact, all you really need to be is great at hunting down the perfect ingredients."

One thing this guy liked to do was search for things. He really enjoyed scouring the Internet for the rare find and made a very good supplemental income buying and selling things on eBay.

"You know what's in the standard burger," I continued. "Beef, tomato, pickle, lettuce, onion; the bun, of course; the sauce is critical; and the cheese is optional. And personally, I'd barbecue the meat over the best hickory chips I could find." I noticed I had his attention—as I said, this guy liked to eat.

"I agree," he replied.

I could almost hear the wheels spinning in his mind, so I continued. "Divvy up the ingredients. Draw from a hat and limit everyone to a 25-mile radius. You can't expect the person who gets assigned the lettuce to drive 300 miles to the lettuce fields in Salinas."

The following Monday, this guy arrived at the studio and couldn't wait to tell me about his experience in creating the perfect hamburger over the weekend. Apparently, he had taken on the role of team leader and kept in touch with the others by cell phone.

Everybody had succeeded in obtaining the perfect ingredients: the pickles were found in a Jewish delicatessen located in the Fairfax district; the tomatoes were discovered in someone's backyard garden and picked fresh off the vine; the buns were baked by someone else's grandmother and came hot out of the oven. This guy told similar great stories of how all the other ingredients were found. When he finally stopped to catch his breath, I asked, "So how was the burger?"

"What?" The question seemed to throw him.

"The *hamburger*. Did you succeed in creating the perfect one?"

"Maybe. Well, I guess so," he said. "It was the best burger I ever tasted, I can tell you that much."

"You see, it wasn't reaching the goal that you found so exciting, it was striving for the goal," I explained.

He smiled and said, "That's right! Now that you say it that way, I can see it."

"Do you think that you can harness that same drive and apply it to today's training?"

"I can try. You bet I can."

That was the key—over the next six months, that student found other ways to tap in to that drive for perfection, and he had great fun doing it. Eventually, he was able to turn that mode on and off at will. He could do it with the most simple obstacles in his life, and also the most difficult.

You can do the same thing. Pick a simple project that you know you can complete and, at the same time, have fun doing. Perhaps you'd like to grow the perfect dozen roses or restore an old silver teapot—I'm sure that you can come up with ten interesting possibilities. Whatever you decide, launch into the task and give it your very best. When you're done, place the result in front of you and cherish the moment while you think back to the mind-set that drove you throughout the process of creating the finished product.

Repeat this process several times a year, increasing the level of difficulty with each new task. Soon you'll be able to switch this mind-set on and off and apply it to areas of your life that will reap substantial benefits. And incidentally, this is a fun exercise to do with your kids!

Define Your Priorities

It is true that the quality of your life will be determined by how accurate you are in defining your priorities. There are just so many hours in a day, and where and how you choose to spend your time really does define what you feel is important in your life. Chances are, if you're like many other people, you're spending far too much time on how you're being presented to the physical world—the home you live in; the company you work for; the size of your bank account; the car you drive; the clothes and jewelry you wear; your hair, nails, teeth, and tan.

My priorities were totally out of whack when I was running those seven martial arts studios in Sin Kil Dong. Over time, I became far too focused on my exterior image. Instead of *living* the life of a master for myself, I became obsessed with *being* the master to others. Master Ko's wise decision to send me to a place where no one cared that I was a master of the martial arts eventually brought my priorities back in line.

Learn to Complete Tasks

A major component of accuracy is completion. Because my martial arts studio is located in the heart of the CBS Studio Center, I teach many extremely gifted creative people—musicians, actors, screenwriters, and even the head of the studio. Over time I've asked these people what they feel separates them from the thousands of other creative people who come to Hollywood every year in search of fame and fortune. Without exception, they have all given me the same answer: What has singled them out from the others is that they have the ability to complete tasks, while dozens of their friends and colleagues had piles of unfinished songs and screenplays that were set aside and never finished. The lesson here is that you can have an abundance of talent, but if you don't have the ability to finish what you start, that talent will go to waste.

We all know people whose lives are cluttered with dozens of unfinished projects, many of which have been lying around for months, even years. If you're one of these people, then I can tell you that the problem you're having is: (1) You have too many projects going at one time, and/or (2) the level of difficulty of the projects you've started is too high.

The solution is to either cut back on the number of projects you have going or start taking on projects that you know you can complete within a reasonable period of time.

Determine Whether Those Unfinished Tasks Are Serving a Hidden Purpose

The biggest problem a person creates when they awaken each day to a never-ending supply of unfinished projects is a lack of time. These projects are like a sponge that absorbs so much of one's energy that *nothing* gets done.

Sometimes an individual who is strapped with all these projects has chosen to keep them in place because they serve as a distraction and an excuse for not relating to others. The person doesn't have enough time to spend with his or her spouse or children or aging parents because all this work is piled up, none of the kids have clean socks, the garbage disposal is stuck again, the spice rack needs to be alphabetized, and the gutters have to be cleaned out before the first storm hits. . . .

If you're using dozens of unfinished projects as a distraction, then you need to look inside yourself and ask *why* you're avoiding your relationships. Is it really all that important to spend four hours washing and waxing your car this weekend, or would that time be better spent with your child? Is shopping at the crowded mall all afternoon really more important than visiting with a sick friend? Are the household chores and projects that you have going all weekend *really* that important?

Practice, Practice, Practice

Committing yourself to a particular goal and agreeing to passionately pursue it are of little value if you don't have persistence. After studying the martial arts for more than a year, I failed my first promotion four times. With my head lowered and feeling distraught, I went to the master and asked, "Master, can I ever pass?"

He looked at me and said, "You have to test yourself first. Do *you* think you can pass?"

I said, "Sir, I thought I was ready, but every time I go out there, I forget all the moves. I feel so ashamed."

He placed his hand on my shoulder and spoke the words I would hear many times in the years that followed. "Son, your worst enemy is within you. If you want to pass, yes, you can, but you have to train hard. You have three names: first name, Practice; middle name, Practice; last name, Practice."

The road to excellence is paved with persistence. If you truly want to become great at anything, be prepared to practice, practice, and practice some more. I have known many gifted martial artists in my life and, without exception, every one of them attained a high level of proficiency through years of persistent practice.

Be Disciplined

The famous people that I teach all share one thing in common—they are disciplined. If you want to be accomplished, learn to discipline yourself. Through discipline, you will acquire the ability to not only focus, but to stay focused.

My daily workout schedule is intense. I begin each day by running five to ten miles at a six-minute-mile pace . . . and I'm 68 years old. How many people half my age can do that? I can still jump six or seven feet in the air and deliver three precision kicks before landing back on my feet. Several times a week I perform 1,000 kicks. Martial artists in their 20s feel they've done well if they kick 1,000 times in a month.

The reason I can keep up this routine is because I've been doing it religiously for years, and I never stop. Working requires discipline, which I feel is about attitude and goes with determination. You have to awaken each morning knowing that you must fulfill something new.

Discipline is also a form of meditation. When I'm running and kicking, I slip into another frame of mind. The fresh air flowing in and out of my lungs, the surging blood in my veins, and the sweat on my body bring me joy. My emphasis in life is discipline—without it, life means nothing. Discipline will lead to self-confidence and self-respect. Whatever form of practice you pursue, make discipline a major part of the formula, and you'll be amazed at the results you achieve.

3. Timing

The third tool critical to survival is the ability to adapt to life's varying rhythms, or *timing*. You have to know when to speed up, slow down, or stand still. The greatest stand-up comedians have said that the key to comedy is timing: Deliver the punch line a second too early or too late, and the joke isn't nearly as funny. Huge fortunes have come and gone in the stock market simply from good and poor timing. Propose marriage three months too soon, and you may be viewed as too impulsive or even needy; propose too late, and you may get turned down because the person you've proposed to is worried that the two of you aren't on the same page.

Pay Attention to Life's Varying Rhythms

There isn't one rhythm to life, but several. The universe slows down, speeds up, pulsates, and moves in waves, but it never stops. Being in sync with the universe and knowing the various options you have when presented with any particular set of circumstances can make the difference between success and failure. You need to know when to start and stop, and when to go fast and then faster. Sometimes in life you need to gradually speed up, while other times you have to accelerate in an instant! Survival often boils down to timing. What follows are a number of rhythms and responses that I've learned in the martial arts and have also successfully applied to my own life.

When Everything Around You Is Spinning Out of Control, Stand Still

Have you ever been in the middle of a family feud? As the battle rages, people try to convince you to side with them so that they can drag you into the fray—but you're wise to do absolutely nothing. Jumping headlong into these battles is like storming a nest of killer bees with a fly swatter. Instead, you should just stand still, for there's safety in the eye of the storm. Later, when everyone else is defeated by their own exhaustion, *then* you can quietly enter the war-torn battlefield and offer a sound opinion. And guess what? Almost everyone will listen to what you have to say, because through it all, you were the one who kept a level head.

As a child, I chose to stand still when those kids were throwing watermelon rinds and rocks at me. I refused to take part in their emotional outbursts. Afterwards, I spent time by myself on the banks of the Golden River. This time alone allowed me to come to an understanding about the root of the particular problem, and I sought out instruction from Master Ko. Eventually, those kids stopped throwing rocks at me and took their anger elsewhere.

The ability to stand still is the job of your guard who holds vigil at the entrance to your mind garden. The guard's task is not to allow high emotion to come in and run rampant. Shakespeare talked about standing still when he wrote the famous phrase "To be or not to be." To me, this is the definition of Taoism—you're there, but you're not there. Standing still is a state of being that is devoid of emotion. Only when you have achieved this state can logic and common sense serve you well.

Go with the Flow

When you simply can't buck the universe—for example, if you're driving through Kansas in late summer and find yourself confronted by a level-four tornado—then you have to *accept* life on its own terms and "go with the flow."

Several years ago, a student of mine married and headed off to Hawaii for his honeymoon. He was a real sun worshiper and had been talking for weeks about how he planned to divide his leisure time between lying on the beach with his wife and going sailing.

Hours after he arrived, he called me in a rage from his hotel room. "Master Yu, it's Sid. I can't believe it. We landed in the middle of a tropical storm, and it's pouring rain over here!" He went on and on about how his honeymoon had been ruined—what was Hawaii without the sun? His plans for lying on the beach and sailing had gone up in smoke.

I told him to go with the flow.

"Flow? What flow?" he asked. "We're talking Noah's Ark over here. There's no sun!"

"You can't change the weather," I said calmly. "But you can find a way to blend with it. Think about it. I'll be interested in hearing how things come out."

A week later, Sid and his wife arrived home. He didn't have much of a tan, but he talked about having the time of his life. Forced to find another way to enjoy his honeymoon with his new wife, he discovered that the tropical rain forests in Hawaii were far more beautiful when it's raining because all that water intensifies the smell of the vegetation. Much to his surprise, he also discovered that there was snow in Hawaii and did some great skiing. And last, when the company that was going to take him sailing called to cancel his reservation, they suggested that perhaps he'd be interested in going scuba diving instead. Sid had never been scuba diving, but he and his wife took the company up on its offer. The dive turned out to be one of the greatest and most romantic experiences they had during their honeymoon.

Go with the flow. If you know that you can't change what the universe is handing you, find a way to turn that stumbling block into a stepping-stone.

Choose to Move Against the Established Rhythm

Have you ever watched what two professional boxers do at the start of every round? Each moves to the center of the ring, stops just short of his opponent's striking range, and then starts to bounce forward and backward and side to side. What's important to note is that they do this *in unison*—in a sense, they dance together. Even when they strike and block in combinations, most fighters will stay within this previously established rhythm. They'll slow the beat and speed it up, but they'll continue to base their rhythm on the whole notes, so to speak.

What happens when one of the fighters chooses to stop moving in the established rhythm and strikes his opponent in between the beats? It totally frustrates and confuses his opponent. Skilled martial artists and fencing masters call this "broken rhythm." In music, this is similar to what's known as syncopation, where the beats or accents are displaced so that the strong beats become weak, and vice versa. People who unwittingly do this on the dance floor make lousy dancers.

Often when couples find themselves arguing on a regular basis, they seem to establish a mutual time to argue. After they're exhausted, there follows a rest period, after which the arguing resumes. If you find yourself in a similar situation, you have a good chance of breaking this pattern if you elect not to stick with the prescribed time schedule. Instead of arguing at night, rest. If the subject of the disagreement must be continued, then try discussing it in the morning.

I used this tactic to my advantage on the tournament circuit. I'd frustrate my opponent by showing up for the grand championship match 15 minutes late. My opponent would have already arrived and would be playing out the match in his head, planning to make his opening moves according to his prescribed schedule. When I wasn't there to respond, my opponent would return to playing the match in his head. When I finally did arrive, he would be mentally playing out the middle or end of the fight and would now be faced with making his opening moves. My opponents complained vehemently about this tactic, but I never received more than a slap on the wrist. And I won many championship matches using this strategy of displacing my opponents' established rhythm.

Speed Up and Slow Down

When I began to fight in tournaments, I was shocked to find out that I was losing matches because I was going too fast. The judges simply couldn't see my punches. When I forced myself to slow down, I started winning trophies.

We often see this in life with regard to personal relationships. Have you ever been told or told someone else, "Slow down; you're going too fast for me"? These words are sound advice, and if not followed, the relationship will almost certainly be short-lived.

Likewise, that same relationship can come to an end if either party feels that the other is moving too slowly. You may hear (or say), "I'm not getting any younger, you know, and I've already invested three years of my life in this relationship. If you need more time to figure out if you really love me, then you probably don't love me enough and never will."

Likewise, in the business world, employees are often terminated from their jobs for the simple reason that they're not being productive enough. Alternatively, the new employee who produces too much too quickly can find him- or herself facing a horde of disgruntled co-workers. Learning when to speed up and slow down to other people's rhythms can make a major difference in life's outcomes.

Remember That the Patterns of the Universe Are Constantly Changing and Are Often Unpredictable

There's far too much going on in this world for you to be able to predict with any certainty how your life will be in a year, let alone five years from now. In my lifetime, for example, I've seen many of my long-term plans dissolve before my very eyes. I had no way of predicting the outbreak of the Korean War, the onset of being homeless 24 hours after arriving in America, or the death of the martial artist who challenged me at the Golden Master's Award ceremony. All of these events resulted in major changes in my life—I'm sure that you've experienced much of the same in your own.

If you question this statement, you can run a simple test. Take, for example, a five-year period of your life, let's say from January 1992 through January 1997. Think back to January 1, 1992—what did you think your life would be like on New Year's Day, 1997? If you're like most people, your prediction didn't even come close. As John Lennon once observed, "Life is what happens to you when you're busy making other plans."

This is what makes life so exciting—the fact that you must have the ability to adapt to ever-changing rhythms. If you learn to move with them and adapt them to your advantage, then the quality of your life will markedly improve.

Take Action

At an early age, I read a passage written by poet Rabindranath Tagore that said, "The song that I came to sing remains unsung to this day. I have spent many days stringing and unstringing this my instrument. The time has not come true, the words have not been rightly set; only there is the agony of wishing in my heart." From that moment, I became determined not to squander my life away tuning and retuning my instrument. Instead, I set my sights on singing the song that I was destined to sing eons ago.

Over the years, I've met a number of people who expressed an interest in learning the martial arts but never got around to training. One such individual was a likable guy named Frank who worked as a stagehand on one of the CBS television shows. Although Frank never came right out and said so, my sense was that his main interest in training had to do with his weight problem. He would drop by my studio every so often to fill me in on how things were going and why he wouldn't be signing up for classes for another month or two. There was always some problem that kept him from getting started.

After several months of this, I decided to do something. Frank and I were talking casually for a while, when I began to delve further into why he still hadn't started his training. "Frank, I have three simple questions I'd like to ask you. I think they'll cut straight through to the problem you're having getting started with the training."

"Sure," he replied. "Go ahead."

"First—do you think that you have a problem with your weight?" I asked.

Frank glanced up at the ceiling in thought, then looked at me and said, "Yeah, I do."

"Okay. Second question—would you like to do something about it?"

Again, Frank paused to think, and then responded, "Yeah, I would."

"Fine. Third question—*when?*"

This time Frank didn't give the question any thought, but instead launched into a string of excuses: The holidays were just around the corner—his wife's mother would be hurt if he didn't have his usual third helping of her sweet potato casserole, followed by her mouth-watering pecan pie; the television show at CBS would be finishing up, which meant a catered wrap party; the first of the year would be all right—after the NFL playoffs and Super Bowl parties with fellow fans. Frank planned on getting started on the first of February, but I knew it wasn't going to happen until he changed his basic thinking.

A wise man once said that procrastination is the thief of time. Truer words were never spoken. Most people who face similar issues like Frank's will readily admit that they have a problem and that they would like to do something about it. Their only stumbling block is making the decision as to *when* they're going to *take action.*

My philosophy is that once you've acknowledged that the problem exists and you're willing to do something to correct it, you should take action *immediately*—not next week, next month, or next year. Do it now. Hesitation and excuse-making are counterproductive. Whatever the problem is that you face, it isn't going to get any better over time. And the longer you put off taking action, the more you sabotage your will to make a positive change in your life.

Preplay/Replay

Back in the early 1980s when personal computers became available, they weren't nearly as efficient as they are today. One of the main problems was that they came with small monitors that didn't allow the user to see more than a third of a standard page at one time. As a result, if you were printing a ten-page document, you had to scroll up and down through the entire file and come up with your best guess as to how the text and margins were going to line up on the pages. Then you'd hit the print key, and what came out was rarely what you had envisioned. As a result, you had to go back into the document and do a whole lot of fixing. Sometimes it would take three or four printings of the same document before everything was right, causing a waste of ink, paper, and time.

Today this problem no longer exists because all the popular word-processing software includes a function known as "print preview." Now, with one click of your mouse, you can preview exactly what each page of the document will look like before you hit the print key.

I use a similar technique that I call "preplay/replay" in life. You, too, can use this sound approach when facing major decisions in your life. For instance, if you're contemplating marriage or divorce, having children, changing jobs, or even undergoing surgery, you can greatly increase your chances of a positive outcome if you simply take the time to first preplay in your mind *all* the relevant facts and circumstances from beginning to end. If, at the conclusion of this exercise, you're pleased with the result, go ahead and replay the scenario in real life. On the other hand, if you don't like what your mind has presented to you as the most logical outcome, then don't proceed with replaying it for real.

Unfortunately, I didn't have this tool in place when I first came to America—I didn't preview what clearly was a major disaster waiting for me in the Golden Land of Opportunity. Back then, I honestly felt that I was going to put my feet on American soil, and the next morning I'd have a job and everything would fall into place. I had no idea that I would be homeless and broke within 24 hours—for I didn't have a plan.

Today I preplay/replay all major decisions in my life by gathering all the facts and playing out the scenario in my mind. If I approve of what appears to be the most logical outcome, then I go ahead and replay in real time what I've already seen in preplay.

4. Power

Finally, to make it through life, you need *power,* which includes physical strength as well as health. The person who doesn't have the strength and endurance to flee from a burning building, or whose physical and mental energy has been depleted by illness, will be ineffective in life.

You Get One Vehicle in Life, and There Are No Trade-Ins

Your body is the vehicle that will carry you along your journey for your entire life. It's what delivers the food and water to your mind garden. And it's the only vehicle you're going to get—if you don't take care of your health, sooner or later you will end up seriously ill. Then you will learn the true meaning of the word *dis-ease,* because there will no longer be anything easygoing about your life.

During the 18 months that I lived on the streets of San Francisco as Monkey Man, I came as close to death as I ever want to come. Near the end, I was coughing up blood, and my liver had swelled to twice its normal size. I felt as if I were 100 years old—I could barely make it up a flight of stairs without struggling to catch my breath; and I lived with chest pains, throbbing headaches, and eyes that lacked clarity. The night that I straddled the Golden Gate Bridge, I honestly felt as if I were about to throw a body into the water that was already dead. I was a walking corpse. You can bet that I rejoiced the day that my body returned to its natural state of robust health.

God meant for you to dance joyously in the sunlight, like Maria on that mountaintop in *The Sound of Music.* To me, there is no greater feeling than getting up in the morning and running ten miles. And after 62 years of training in the martial arts, I still get excited about putting on my uniform, kicking the bags, and running through the forms. This is what makes me happy.

You don't have to become a health fanatic or a fitness guru to start feeling healthier. You know better than anyone where those red flags are in your daily routine that will ultimately undermine your health. Pay attention to them. They're waving in front of your eyes for a reason. Don't wait until your ship is halfway sunk before you decide to start bailing water.

Would you like to have a three-week vacation every year that costs nothing? Start taking better care of yourself, and you'll find that you need an hour less sleep. Over the year, that extra waking hour will add up to more than three weeks. Just think what you could do with an extra three weeks of free time!

Do Everything with Passion

Passion is one of the greatest aspects of your self. Whatever you do, put every bit of your heart and soul into the task in front of you. Take pride in everything that's an expression of you. The act is empowering.

When I was washing dishes, I did the best job I could. As a result, no one ever sent a dish back to the kitchen because it wasn't clean enough. I prided myself on being able to see the reflection of my face in every dish I washed. The silverware that left me was as clean as a fork or spoon that I would have placed before my mother and father. I was never ashamed of being a dishwasher, because a clean stack of dishes was merely the result—the real me was the expression of passion that I put into the washing. And that feeling was no different than the passion Leonardo da Vinci felt when he painted the Mona Lisa.

Think Things Through

When I was living on a shoestring budget in Berkeley in the mid-1960s, I should have thought ahead before spending my last $300 on that '56 Chevy convertible. But I really wanted it. I *had* to have it. And when the owner kept telling me that the car had problems, I just didn't hear it.

In the end, not only did I have to say good-bye to my dream car at a junkyard, but I faced a string of tickets and a tongue-lashing from an angry judge. I could have saved myself (and others) a whole lot of trouble had I simply taken the time to think this though. So, before you make the mistake of allowing your heated passion to lead you into a similar nightmare, run the scenario through preplay/replay. If the result looks good, then you can replay it in real time.

Understand That Words Have Power

When I was a child growing up in Korea, I was totally defenseless because of my physical and mental disabilities. The kids in my neighborhood took advantage of me because they thought it was fun. But even when they were throwing rocks at my head, I kept thinking, *These are my friends. This doesn't hurt that much. It's okay. This pain will only last for a few minutes, but these kids are going to be my friends forever.*

To this day, I can still recall the faces of some of those boys who hit me and said mean things to me. I can especially recall when the doctor told my parents that they should put me in a corner to die, as well as when Master K told me that I was a loser and a quitter.

I'm sure that there are times when you've lost your temper and said things out of anger that you didn't mean. Yet you should always try to remember that you have the potential of unleashing an incredibly destructive power from your mouth that's far more devastating than physical violence. Cruel words have the power to scar another person for life, especially a child. Tragically, some words can never be forgotten, because there simply is no eraser big enough. So while I teach a physical art comprised of kicks and punches, I teach my students to discipline themselves with regard to what comes out of their mouths as well.

By the same token, words spoken in kindness are more valuable than diamonds and gold. And as a prelude to speaking such niceties, always remember that two of your greatest physical assets are your handshake and your smile.

Also keep in mind that actions almost always speak louder than words. How often do you say "I love you" to someone? When you do, is it because saying the words has become a matter of habit, or do you truly mean it? And do they respond "I love you, too" in the same tone and enthusiasm that they use when they ask for the television remote control? Words without action are meaningless. Just saying "I love you" doesn't mean much if you don't take action that demonstrates your love for that person. If you love someone, you *do* things for them.

Learn to Be a Good Listener

The flip side of speaking power is listening power. One of the greatest gifts that you can give to someone you care about (especially your children) is to be a good listener—I cannot emphasize this enough.

I believe that the first time in my life I ever truly listened to the gut feelings of another human being was the night that Ronny and I talked together on Fisherman's Wharf. That night was the first time I honestly ever felt connected to another human being.

So many people in this life have never really been listened to. As a result, they live in a lonely silence with thoughts that no one else knows and feelings that no one else can share.

How often have you had the experience of trying to talk to people, but instead of their hearing what you're saying, it's obvious that they're just waiting for you to pause long enough so they can interject their own feelings, advice, and thoughts?

People have an inner sense about when someone isn't truly listening. Often they don't say anything because—well, the other person isn't listening. Learning to be a good listener takes considerable practice. But if you can become good at it, you'll find that your friends and loved ones—and even strangers—will be drawn to your presence. Being a good listener is a rare gift, and one of the most important ones you'll ever possess.

chapter 16 :::
Keys
to
Success

:::
:::

Ultimately, whatever your goals are in life, you need three things in order to become successful: desire, ability, and opportunity. If you're missing any one of these, you won't become a success. For instance, if you have desire but lack ability, when opportunity comes, it will pass you by; if you have ability but no desire, the opportunity won't end in a positive result; or if you have desire and opportunity but lack ability, you won't be a success. There's just no getting around the fact that you need all three.

The Pyramid of Success

Imagine that the success you're trying to achieve sits at the top of a three-level pyramid. The foundation, or first level, is represented by what I refer to as *the three D's*—**D**esire, **D**etermination, and **D**iscipline.

These things are developed through the mind and are crucial to your success. Moreover, each leads to the next. In other words, whatever your goal is in life, you must first ask yourself if you truly possess a strong desire to attain that goal. Remember, *that which you are seeking is causing you to seek.* If you don't feel strongly about the goal and can't become emotionally overwhelmed by a mental image of your having finally achieved it, then there's a strong possibility that you're on the wrong road.

If, however, you find that this mental image evokes a burning need within you, then harness that desire and let it lead you to acquiring an intense and unstoppable determination. With these two qualities in place, developing discipline simply becomes a matter of reporting for duty every day while constantly telling yourself, "No matter what, I will not quit!"

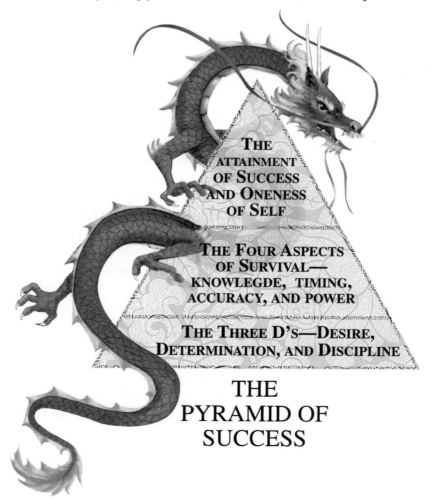

THE
ATTAINMENT
OF SUCCESS
AND ONENESS
OF SELF

THE FOUR ASPECTS
OF SURVIVAL—
KNOWLEGDE, TIMING,
ACCURACY, AND POWER

THE THREE D'S—DESIRE,
DETERMINATION, AND DISCIPLINE

THE
PYRAMID OF
SUCCESS

Once you have the positive mind-set of desire, determination, and discipline, you're ready to proceed to the middle level of the pyramid. This level comprises the four aspects of survival, which I talked about in Chapter 15: knowledge, timing, accuracy, and power.

And finally, the top of the pyramid is the attainment of success and a oneness of self. This oneness is a blending of one's mind, body, and spirit—and its only by-product is *wisdom,* which I defined earlier as the proper use of knowledge, and the only thing that you'll take with you when you die.

The Golden Principles of Life

Throughout your journey, and on all levels of your climb to the top of this pyramid, apply the following "Golden Principles": *Be mindful of where you've been, where you are today, and where you're going; stick to basics; and follow through.*

The Golden Principles will maintain your forward progress as you continue along the road to success. To put it all together: (1) At all times you should watch the road—that is, be clear on where you came from and where you're heading; (2) stick to basics by applying the three D's (desire, determination, and discipline) and the four key aspects needed for survival (knowledge, timing, accuracy, and power); and (3) follow through (no matter what, refuse to quit!).

Whatever hardships and obstacles come your way, as long as you put forth your best effort and follow these basic principles—if mentally, physically, and spiritually you continue to move closer to becoming one with yourself—then you can *only* come out a winner.

Besides these basic principles, I strongly encourage you to develop the following abilities in yourself, which are absolutely critical to your leading a happy life.

The Ability to Forgive

Perhaps the greatest power on the face of the earth is the ability you have to forgive yourself and others. With few exceptions, people don't do and say hurtful things because they want to—they do it because they're carrying so much baggage on their backs that they become crushed beneath the emotional weight.

It took me a long time to forgive the people in my life who I felt had wronged me. Collectively, they made up a formidable group: the doctor who handed me a death sentence; those kids who tormented me as a child; the hundreds of soldiers who shot at me during the Korean War; the hotel clerk who greeted my arrival in America by calling me a "lousy foreigner"; and Master K, who called me a quitter and a loser—just to name a few. However, I ultimately came to recognize that Master Ko hadn't taught me his beloved art so that I could walk through life being a bully.

When someone wrongs you, don't continue to punish them to relieve your own anger and frustration. And don't destroy a valued friendship, family relationship, or marriage over one or two wrong deeds or string of harsh words.

I often equate forgiveness with my own mind garden when I'm reminded of these profoundly compassionate words of Mark Twain: "Forgiveness is the fragrance the violet sheds on the heel that has crushed it."

If you can find a way in hurtful times to become a violet in your own mind garden, you'll make this world a better place for yourself and those around you.

The Ability to Let Go of Anger

There's nothing more destructive to your physical health and peace of mind than holding on to anger. There are far too many people in this world who have made a career of this—but tragically, the ones they're hurting the most are themselves.

The day those kids threw watermelon rinds and rocks at me, my feelings were hurt and I was angry; by nightfall, that anger turned to hatred. What I didn't understand at the time was that this was *my* hatred—I owned it and carried it around with me wherever I went. I'd given these kids permission not only to hurt me once, but to continue to control my feelings. This negativity impacted my spirit while the kids went about their lives as they always had, totally unaware of my miserable state. As long as I continued to blame them for the way I felt, I had to wait for them to change before I could let go of my anger and hatred. Ultimately, I came to see the error of my thinking and just let go of all that ill will. Almost overnight, I began to feel much better.

The Ability to Cherish Your God-Given Ability to Cry

Charles Dickens once wisely wrote: "Heaven knows we need never be ashamed of our tears." Unfortunately, in both the American and Asian cultures, crying is often looked upon as weakness, particularly in men. I don't agree with this. Crying is a natural process—I began my life as a "crying baby," and I've allowed myself to cry for 68 years. I cried when that restaurant manager gave me the dishwashing job, and I openly wept several times during the writing of this book. Crying is one aspect of our nature that separates us from the rest of the animal kingdom. I believe that God had a good reason for giving us this unique ability—crying is a medicine that soothes our spirit and restores locked energy.

It's important that you have a place to go to where you can cry. Go there whenever you feel the need to shed a tear, and bawl as hard and for as long as you can. There's no greater way to release pent-up anger than to cry. Of course, it's best if you can do so in the arms of one who truly cares about you—but if this is unavailable, go to your special place and cry to the universe. God will meet you there and rock you in His arms.

The Ability to Laugh

Besides your power to cry, God gave you the unique ability to laugh. No other member of the animal kingdom is able to laugh or has a sense of humor. A child who falls from his bicycle almost always has one of two reactions—he or she either laughs or cries, as both serve as a release of negative energy. Have you ever watched a child laugh and cry at the same time? It's beautiful.

Many years ago, there was a man who had been diagnosed with terminal cancer. Determined not to live out his final days in a state of depression and despair, he set up a projector in his bedroom and ran old comedic movies nonstop for a month. After watching hundreds of hours of Laurel and Hardy, Buster Keaton, Charlie Chaplin, W.C. Fields, and The Three Stooges, the man was restored to health. His cancer miraculously disappeared.

Like tears, laughter is a medicine that soothes the spirit and can heal a body stricken with disease, so take the time to continually develop and nurture a strong sense of humor. Get into the habit of now and again not taking yourself so damn seriously. Laugh often and loud, and have fun with life. I can assure you that life will surely have fun with you.

The Ability to Give Only Good to the Universe

If the only thing that you put into the universe is good, then that's the only thing you can get back. After all, you can't plant radishes and get cucumbers. When I see students expressing ill will, or even downright hatred for another person, I tell them that such actions are akin to throwing a ball at a solid wall—if they throw the ball as hard as possible, it will most assuredly come back with the same force and hit them in the face. So the harder they throw, the harder the ball will come back.

This is a cold law of the universe. If what you give out is hatred and unkind words and vengefulness, always selfishly looking out for number one, then you're going to receive the same. If, however, what you give to the universe is love, kindness, compassion, and forgiveness, then that's what you'll receive in return.

The Ability to Develop a Positive Attitude

Finally, Henry Thoreau once said that a man is rich in proportion to the number of things he can let alone. In other words, you should be happy and content with what you have. This isn't to say that there's anything wrong with working hard to improve your lifestyle. Just don't get caught up in the rut of chasing material possessions. You came into this world with nothing but your physical body, and that's how you'll leave. I have yet to see a hearse with a trailer hitch.

It is in the spirit of love that I offer you, the reader, all that's contained in this book, and I wish you great success.

Afterword

When I was ten years old, life went by at ten miles per hour. It just seemed to take forever for me to reach my next birthday, and I wanted to get older in a hurry. When I turned 20, life sped up a bit to about 20 miles per hour, and from there ran increasingly faster—30, 40, 50, 60. Now that I'm 68 years of age, my life is running at 68 miles per hour—which is slightly over the freeway speed limit in most states! Everything in my life now seems to be racing by at breakneck speed.

I feel blessed and honored that Master Ko was such a major part of my journey. I was always willing to sacrifice everything for him, no matter how big or small. In return, the martial arts that he taught me have allowed me to conquer all my obstacles in life and ultimately fulfill my destiny.

Most of all, for more than 60 years I've experienced the sheer joy of learning, training, and teaching the martial arts. Of these three, I've valued the learning process the most because it was during my learning years that I was the closest to Master Ko. This is why I often say that if I could spend another year with him, I'd be willing to give up whatever remaining time I have left on Earth. That's how much I valued the joy of learning the martial arts from my master.

I am an extremely fortunate man. My job is *teaching* the martial arts, and my hobby is *training* in the martial arts, and I get to do both in one place—my studio at CBS Studio Center, which isn't far from my home. Because I've been able to incorporate the basic principles of the martial arts into my life, today I'm someone who knows who and what he is.

After reading this book, you know that my journey hasn't been easy. Along the way, I've had many crosses to bear and faced countless obstacles. But I accepted the challenges, and just kept telling myself over and over what the master always told me: *Do not be a quitter and a loser.*

Because I believed in my heart that the universe wanted me to achieve my goal and fulfill my destiny, I labored ahead and learned many of life's most valuable lessons in the process. What a joy this journey has been, and continues to be.

I would like to close by taking a few moments to talk about my art. My mission is nowhere near complete—there's still more work to do. I feel that Tae Kwon Do has gone too far in the direction of "sport." There's much more to Tae Kwon Do than sport. The "Do" of the art is defined as "The Way," which is the daily *living* aspect of the art, not necessarily the self-defense aspect. Among other things, the "Do" includes internal power, breathing exercises, form, and meditation. It's a part of the art that reaches the inner spirit, and if we, as martial artists, continue to focus too heavily on the sports side of Tae Kwon Do, the deep spiritual side of the art will die out, and we'll lose 4,700 years of highly revered traditions and customs.

Students who want more than "sport Tae Kwon Do" must become professionals rather than focusing on the amateur side. They must make the art their life, as I have. They must *live* the art instead of just practicing techniques and competing in tournaments.

Unfortunately, too many of today's instructors and masters are more interested in material gain than they are in taking the art to the highest level of inner peace and love. They're more attracted to external things such as driving a nice car, living in a big house, wearing designer clothes, and eating at trendy restaurants. Granted, one can argue that such an attitude is human nature, but my feeling is that if these instructors aren't willing to put a premium on the higher levels of the martial arts, then they should go into some other business.

I realize that Tae Kwon Do instructors and masters are living in changing times—after all, the potential student pool isn't what it was 20 years ago. Today, many instructors view students over the age of 15 as too old to take up Tae Kwon Do. The reason is simple: Because of their work schedules, most adults can only train in limited evening classes, which represent about 15 percent of the school's enrollment. The remaining 85 percent is made up of children, who are brought in substantial numbers by their parents. These kids train in the mornings and afternoons, Monday through Saturday. Because of their large and consistent numbers, children can be likened to the slot machines that pay the rent on the huge Las Vegas casinos. If these casinos had to rely on the high rollers to pay the rent, they would soon go out of business.

As a result, what we have today are hordes of parents signing up their young children—and when these kids reach the age of 12 or 13, most of them drop out and take up soccer or Little League. So, because children aren't taught the deep spiritual side of the art, higher levels of Tae Kwon Do are dying out.

Another major area that I'm determined to address is the manner in which the martial arts are depicted in motion pictures and television. This is the main reason why I moved to Los Angeles and why I'm personally teaching so many creative people. I'm trying to educate them about the deeper aspects of the martial arts. So much of what the public sees today represents only the physical side of the art.

Hollywood needs more screenwriters and directors who are also skilled martial artists. Unfortunately, they can't get onto the screen what they personally have no experience of. The art that the public is seeing today is watered down and painful for me to watch. Correcting this—connecting the internal and spiritual aspects of the physical side—is something I've taken on as my personal duty.

As a responsible martial arts community, we need to find a way to reverse these trends. If we don't, we risk losing all of the hard work that was put forth centuries ago by our founding fathers—countless masters who tried as best they could to attain the highest levels of our ancient art. The sacrifice that these men gave for our benefit is like a river of sweat heading for the ocean: If we don't reverse these trends, this river will stop somewhere and dry up. The public deserves much more than the sport side of Tae Kwon Do, and I am committed for the rest of my days to working toward achieving that end. One day at a time—one more step in running, one more punch, one more kick toward achieving that end.

The martial arts have been my life. When the end finally comes for me, I don't want to die in my home or at a hospital. I want to die in my studio, wearing my uniform with my black belt tied around my waist. I want to have a little sweat on my face when I look up from the mats at a group of my best students, also dressed in uniform. I would like my last breath to be taken with a smile, and then I will go.

If I'm to be remembered by a single sentence, it would be: "Don't give up, because if I can do it, you can do it!" Until it's my time to go, I will continuously fight to be a candle that lights the way along a path leading to knowledge and truth—and I'll do so in a spirit of love and caring and sharing.

While Master Ko was alive, I often said, "The master's wish is my command." Of all his wishes, the most important was that I become a better person each and every day of my life. Now it's *my* turn to pass down to my students the knowledge that Master Ko gave me. This is the only way that I can truly repay my master. I remember he always said, "If you think I am good, I want you to be great. Make your students better than you. This is how you can pay me back."

After more than 60 years of training in the martial arts, these words form the philosophy of my teaching. Above all else, I put forth my best effort with a strong passion. This I do out of a deep sense of gratitude and loyalty to my master, who in his lifetime gave me a whole lot more than I ever gave him.

I wish you well and hope that what's contained in this book will greatly enrich your life. If I can be of service to you in any way, please do not hesitate to contact me at: **www.ByongYu.com.**

About the Authors

Born in 1935, **Grandmaster Byong Yu** was raised in Korea and later moved to the United States in 1964. Overcoming physical disabilities, language barriers, racial prejudice, and homelessness, Master Yu took the martial arts circuit by storm and eventually attained the highest rank of black belt (9th degree) from the World Tae Kwon Do Federation. He was voted "Man of the Century" by the Martial Arts Masters' Association, and in 2001 received the prestigious "Martial Arts World Federation Lifetime Achievement Award."

Master Yu presently resides in the Los Angeles area, where, at the age of 68, he continues to teach martial arts at his studio located inside the CBS Studio Center in Studio City. His life story is currently being chronicled in a full-length feature film project entitled *Monkey Man*.

Tom Bleecker began his writing career in 1969 as a screenwriter for director Blake Edwards. After nearly two decades writing for screen and television, in 1987 Bleecker co-authored his first book with Linda Lee: *The Bruce Lee Story,* which served as the source material for MCA Universal's motion picture *Dragon: The Bruce Lee Story*. In 1996, Bleecker wrote a second book on Lee, a highly controversial bestseller entitled *Unsettled Matters*. His most current work is *The Journey,* which features two dozen of America's most prominent martial artists. Bleecker lives in Southern California, where he's currently writing a motion picture scheduled to be filmed in Prague in 2004.

NOTES

NOTES

notes

notes

NOTES

notes

NOTES

notes

We hope you enjoyed this Hay House book.
If you would like to receive a free catalog featuring additional
Hay House books and products, or if you would like information about
the Hay Foundation, please contact:

Hay House, Inc.
P.O. Box 5100
Carlsbad, CA 92018-5100

(760) 431-7695 or **(800) 654-5126**
(760) 431-6948 (fax) or **(800) 650-5115 (fax)**
www.hayhouse.com

Published and distributed in Australia by:
Hay House Australia, Ltd., 18/36 Ralph St., Alexandria NSW 2015
Phone: 612-9669-4299 • *Fax:* 612-9669-4144
www.hayhouse.com.au

Published and Distributed in the United Kingdom by:
Hay House UK, Ltd. • Unit 202, Canalot Studios
222 Kensal Rd., London W10 5BN
Phone: 44-20-8962-1230 • *Fax:* 44-20-8962-1239
www.hayhouse.co.uk

Distributed in Canada by:
Raincoast • 9050 Shaughnessy St., Vancouver, B.C. V6P 6E5
Phone: (604) 323-7100 • *Fax:* (604) 323-2600

Sign up via the Hay House USA Website to receive the Hay House online
newsletter and stay informed about what's going on with your favorite authors.
You'll receive bimonthly announcements about: Discounts and Offers, Special
Events, Product Highlights, Free Excerpts, Giveaways, and more!